Advance Predictive Techniques of
ASHTAKVARGA

Advance Predictive Techniques of
ASHTAKVARGA

by

M. S. Mehta
&
Rajesh C. Dadwal

Sagar Publications

72, Janpath, Ved Mansion
New Delhi-110001
Tel.: 23320648, 23328245
E-mail: sagarpub@del3.vsnl.net.in
Website: www.sagarpublications.com

First Edition 2007
Reprint 2012

Published and printed by Saurabh Sagar for Sagar Publications New Delhi-110001 and printed at The Artwaves, A-487, Ground Floor, Double Storey, Kalkaji, New Delhi-110019, Telfax.: 41609709

About the Authors

The authors of the book **M.S. Mehta** and **Rajesh C. Dadwal** are Faculty Members of the school of Astrology of **Bhartiya Vidya Bhavan**, which is the largest school of astrology in the world. They have many years of teaching experience and have taught hundred of students the advanced techniques of predictions. Under their guidance students have learnt the art of prediction with ease and comfort.

This book is the result of long years of teaching experience and hopefully will provide new material for interpretations of horoscopes.

M.S. Mehta has already written many books on Astrology which include **'Planets and Foreign Travels'**, **'Analysing Horoscopes through Modern Techniques'** and **'Varsha Phala'** etc. under the guidance of K.N. Rao. He has also written many articles on Mundane Astrology for prestigious **'Journal of Astrology'**.

Acknowledgment

This book which contains advanced techniques in prediction of Ashtakvarga would not have been possible but for the active support by **the students** and **faculty members** of **Bhartiya Vidya Bhavan**. It is they who have provided us with data and material to complete the book. We are specially thankful to Deepa Gupta who have provided active moral and typing assistance in completing this book.

We are thankful to Pawan Thapliyal for his efforts to collect the material and to translate for hindi edition.

We also indebted to Dr. (Mrs.) Rama Mishra for going through this book in minutest details and giving us many useful suggestions. Our special thanks are due to Narinder and Saurabh Sagar for taking great pains in bringing out this book so promptly and in such an elegant manner.

Preface

Astrology is a divine science and for accurate predictions grace of gurus and gods is necessary.

Our Guru **K.N. Rao** had guided us in to the right path and divine help has come in many forms in the shape of new material on Ashtakvarga which has not so far been published in any book.

Ashtakvarga is a unique system to assess the strength of Bhavas and planets and provided guidance for giving accurate predictions. To give an example, a well placed Sun in the horoscope will take a person to dizzy heights. Person with such a Sun will be a born leader and success would come to him easily. Since in natural zodiac Sun is Karka of the fifth house, the house of *Poorva Punya*, success and high intelligence, it is not possible to achieve high status and success in life without a strong Sun. Similarly a strong Moon will make a person a great humanitarian with interest in public welfare and a great peace of mind. With afflicted and weak Moon a person does not have a proper thinking capacity and is prone to dull and morose life.

It is only Ashtakvarga that will tell us about the strength and weakness of planets and ultimately the periods of happiness prosperity or turmoil and dejections.

Great contribution of Ashtakvarga is that it gives at a glance picture of strength and weakness of the horoscope and provides best guidance for remedial measures.

Ashtakvarga system is not there in any other branch of Astrology of the world and provides a convincing proof that divine science of Astrology took birth in India which is the land of *Rishis & Munis*.

CONTENTS

Chapter 1

Ashtakvarga System of Prediction

What is Ashtakvarga?

Asht means eight. Ashtakvarga means eight *Vargas* (i.e. divisions or parts). These are Lagna and 7 planets. It signifies eight types of influences exerted on a planet with reference to itself, from Lagna and six other planets, (there are 7 planets in all, Sun, Moon, Mars Mercury, Jupiter, Venus and Saturn which are considered. - Rahu and Ketu being shadowy planets are ignored). Normally transit of a planet is seen from Lagna or from Moon. However, its relative position with reference to itself and other planets are ignored. Ashtakvarga removes this deficiency. This is the combined effect of energies of all the eight exerted on a planet while it is in transit. It is a common knowledge that a planet in transit may be in a benefic position from Moon but may or may not be in a benefic position with respect to Lagna and other seven planets including itself. Ashtakvarga shows the sum total of influences whether for good or bad of all the planets. **In nutshell it shows the strength of a planet in transit. (A strong planet whether malefic or benefic gives good results while a corresponding weak planet gives evil results.)**

Importance of Ashtakvarga:

Prithyuasas, son of Varahamihira, in his book Horasara has said "While general results on the basis of transit can be known, the finer results can only be had from the use of Ashtakvarga." According to him even though there may be bad Yogas in the horoscope like Yogas for widowhood or *Vaidhavya Yoga* and Yogas for loss of daughters, *Kanya Kshyaya*, these Yogas will not give bad results if Jupiter's Ashtakvarga is strong. Hence the importance of study of Ashtakvarga.

Again according to the same author, "Among the systems of *Ayurdaya*, Ashtakvarga is the best. The longevity should be evaluated through Ashtakvarga system when the Moon is in Kendra and in the company of a planet while the 10th house has both benefics and malefic."

Ashtakvarga is a unique system developed by the genius of Hindu *Maharishis* to assess the strength of planets in transit. The birth horoscope shows only the positions of planets at the time of birth, but since planets are in motion all the time with respects to their original position as well as with reference to other planets it is necessary to establish the strength of the planets to ascertain whether they will give good or bad results. It is established rule of astrology that only strong planets can give good results, for example a strong Sun in the horoscope will give high status, respect, wealth and good health while a weak Sun will lead to being discarded by family and friends. There will be quarrels with bosses leading to disgrace. There will also be a heart problem and 'aimless wandering' as Parashara calls it. It is for this reason that Phaladeepika extols the virtue of a third system with whose help one can establish whether the planet will give good or evil results. And according to Parashara only general predictions can be given on the basis of birth horoscope, definite results can only be ascertained with the help of Ashtakvarga. This system therefore, is an offshoot of Parashari system and provides a great aid to give accurate predictions.

Malefic Influences of Planets Contributing Zero to a Rashi

Each planet signifies a certain aspect and are called Sthira Karakas. Malefic influence of any planet will be on their particular natural Karakatwas, e.g. Sun - father; Moon - mother; Mars - co-borns; Mercury - Gyati/relatives (uncle); Jupiter - Putra; Venus -

Kalatra; Saturn - Servant. Whenever a planet contributes 0 benefic Bindus to a Rashi, it will afflict the native/horoscope in the following ways:

1. The natural Karakatwa of the planet will suffer;

2. It will influence the Lagnadhi Bhava where it has contributed 0. Also the Bhavas owned by that particular planet if he is not placed in either of them, will be afflicted.

3. It will influence or afflict the Kaala Purusha Bhava(s) represented by the Rashi where benefic Bindus are 0.

4. It will influence the Rashi/Bhava where the planet is placed.

5. When a planet owns two Rashis and is placed in one of them, the Rashi where the contribution is 0 will only get afflicted, not the other Rashi.

6. Significations of the planet itself. Eg.: Mars owns the 1st and 8th Bhavas of Kaala Purusha. Thus, he will afflict head, may give head injuries, affect reproductive organs.

7. Transit of malefic like Mars, Saturn, Rahu, Ketu, the planet itself may prove very bad during a bad Dasha/Antardasha. Aspect of benefics in transit will reduce the amount of affliction. If a transiting planet contributing 8 or 7 benefic Bindus gets exalted in the Rashi where another planet has contributed 0, then this will compensate the malefic effects. The planet contributing 0 cannot be taken individually, compensating factors have to be seen in total. The same can be said for the transit of the planet itself who has contributed 0 Bindus in that Rashi.

Some terms that are used in Ashtakvarga system are as follows:

1. **Bindus or Benefic points:** Excluding Rahu and Ketu, each of seven planets, Sun Moon, Mars, Mercury, Jupiter, Venus, Saturn plus Lagna release energies of eight types for good or

for evil. The good or benefic points are known in northern India as *'Bindus'* (points or dots) whereas In South India the benefic points are called *'Rekhas'* or vertical lines. **In this book we will use the term *'Bindus'* for benefic points and *'Rekhas'* for evil points.**

2. **Bhinnashtakvarga** (BAV) or Ashtakvarga of each of seven planets.

3. **Sarvashtakvarga** (SAV) or sum total of Bindus in each of twelve Bhavas. This is also known as Samudayashtakvarga.

4. **Prasthara Chakra:** This is complete picture of sum total of all the Bindus in all the 12 Rashis in a tabulated form as shown in the following pages.

Rekha Sarvashtakvarga:

The total number of benefic and malefic points in a Rashi is always 56. Therefore, if Bindus (benefic points) are deducted from 56 we arrive at the malefic points or *Rekhas* as these are called in northern India. For example if in a horoscope in sign Aries there are 32 Bindus or benefic points then in that Rashi there will be 56 minus 32 or 24 Rekhas. Sarvashtakvarga and Mandal Shodhan of Rekhas are done in a similar manner as that of Bindus.

The benefic places of planets with reference to themselves and seven other planets including Lagna are known as **Bhinnashtakvarga** and are given in a table form on next page.

Construction of Ashtakvarga Charts

This has been explained in Chapter II.

For construction of various charts **Table I** given on the next page would be utilized. This gives the benefic position of each planet with reference to itself, Lagna and other six planets.

Table A

For Sun (48 pts.)

From									Total
Saturn	1	2	4	7	8	9	10	11	8
Jupiter	5	6	9	11					4
Mars	1	2	4	7	8	9	10	11	8
Sun	1	2	4	7	8	9	10	11	8
Venus	6	7	12						3
Mercury	3	5	6	9	10	11	12		7
Moon	3	6	10	11					4
Lagna	3	4	6	10	11	12			6
Total									48

For Moon (49 pts.)

From									Total
Saturn	3	5	6	11					4
Jupiter	1	4	7	8	10	11	12		7
Mars	2	3	5	6	9	10	11		7
Sun	3	6	7	8	10	11			6
Venus	3	4	5	7	9	10	11		7
Mercury	1	3	4	5	7	8	10	11	8
Moon	1	3	6	7	10	11			6
Lagna	3	6	10	11					4
Total									49

For Mars (39 pts.)

From									Total
Saturn	1	4	7	8	9	10	11		7
Jupiter	6	10	11	12					4
Mars	1	2	4	7	8	10	11		7
Sun	3	5	6	10	11				5
Venus	6	8	11	12					4
Mercury	3	5	6	11					4
Moon	3	6	11						3
Lagna	1	3	6	10	11				5
Total									39

For Mercury (54 pts.)

From									Total
Saturn	1	2	4	7	8	9	10	11	8
Jupiter	6	8	11	12					4
Mars	1	2	4	7	8	9	10	11	8
Sun	5	6	9	11	12				5
Venus	1	2	3	4	5	8	9	11	8
Mercury	1	3	5	6	9	10	11	12	8
Moon	2	4	6	8	10	11			6
Lagna	1	2	4	6	8	10	11		7
Total									54

For **Jupiter** (56 pts)

From										Total
Saturn	3	5	6	12						4
Jupiter	1	2	3	4	7	8	10	11		8
Mars	1	2	4	7	8	10	11			7
Sun	1	2	3	4	7	8	9	10	11	9
Venus	2	5	6	9	10	11				6
Mercury	1	2	4	5	6	9	10	11		8
Moon	2	5	7	9	11					5
Lagna	1	2	4	5	6	7	9	10	11	9
Total										56

For **Venus** (52 pts)

From										Total
Saturn	3	4	5	8	9	10	11			7
Jupiter	5	8	9	10	11					5
Mars	3	5	6	9	11	12				6
Sun	8	11	12							3
Venus	1	2	3	4	5	8	9	10	11	9
Mercury	3	5	6	9	11					5
Moon	1	2	3	4	5	8	9	11	12	9
Lagna	1	2	3	4	5	8	9	11		8
Total										52

For **Saturn** (39 pts)

From										Total
Saturn	3	5	6	11						4
Jupiter	5	6	11	12						4
Mars	3	5	6	10	11	12				6
Sun	1	2	4	7	8	10	11			7
Venus	6	11	12							3
Mercury	6	8	9	10	11	12				6
Moon	3	6	11							3
Lagna	1	3	4	6	10	11				6
Total										39

Planets Factor or Graha Gunakar

Planets	Sun	Moon	Mars	Mercury	Jupiter	Venus	Saturn
Units	5	5	8	5	10	7	5

Rashi Factor or Rashi Gunakar

Rashi	1	2	3	4	5	6	7	8	9	10	11	12
Units	7	10	8	4	10	5	7	8	9	5	11	12

TABLE-S

Calculating Sarvashtakvarga without Bhinnashtak & Prasthara Varga

Planets/ Rashis	1	2	3	4	5	6	7	8	9	10	11	12
Saturn	3	2	4	4	4	3	3	4	4	4	6	1
Jupiter	2	1	1	2	3	4	2	4	2	4	7	4
Mars	4	5	3	4	3	3	4	4	4	6	7	2
Sun	3	3	3	3	2	3	4	5	3	5	7	2
Venus	2	3	3	3	4	4	2	3	4	3	6	3
Mercury	3	1	5	2	6	6	1	2	5	5	7	3
Moon	2	3	5	2	2	5	2	2	2	3	7	1
Lagna	5	3	5	5	2	6	1	2	2	6	7	1
Total	24	21	29	25	26	34	19	26	26	36	54	17

Chapter 2

How to make Ashtakvarga Charts

In this scheme of Ashtakvarga eight charts will have to be constructed.

Chart no 1	– Table II - 1	– Prastharashtakvarga of Sun
Chart no 2	– Table II - 2	– Prastharashtakvarga of Moon
Chart no 3	– Table II - 3	– Prastharashtakvarga of Mars
Chart no 4	– Table II - 4	– Prastharashtakvarga of Mercury
Chart no 5	– Table II - 5	– Prastharashtakvarga of Jupiter
Chart no 6	– Table II - 6	– Prastharashtakvarga of Venus
Chart no 7	– Table II - 7	– Prastharashtakvarga of Saturn
Chart no 8	– Table II - 8	– Total of all - Sarvashtakvarga

Rahu and Ketu do not come into picture.

This is illustrated with the horoscope of Mrs. Indira Gandhi, famous late Prime Minister of India

Asd	Sun	Moon	Mars	Mercury
$24^0 18$'	$4^0 07$'	$5^0 35$'	$16^0 22$'	$13^0 13$'

Jupiter	Venus	Saturn	Rahu	Ketu
$15^0 00$'	$21^0 00$'	$21^0 47$'	$9^0 12$'	$9^0 12$'

Method:

Use a blank chart - Table A and mark location of Planets.

Step No. 1

Putting asterisk marks to denote placement of planets as exist in the horoscope.

In Indira Gandhi's horoscope, Saturn is in Cancer; therefore put an asterisk mark in the relevant horizontal column under Rashi Cancer against vertical column Saturn. This asterisk mark would show the **first position** from where counting would begin. Similarly make an asterisk mark for Jupiter in the column under Taurus against planet Jupiter. In the same way asterisk marks should be put for Mars under column Leo against planet Mars, for Sun under column Scorpio against Sun, for Venus under column Sagittarius against Venus, for Mercury under column Scorpio against Mercury; and Moon under Capricorn against Moon. Asterisk for Ascendant would be under Rashi Cancer against column Ascendant. This will take shape as shown in Table A. Now start placing Bindus in the relevant columns with the help of Table 1 -Sun.

Sun's Prastharashtakvarga - Table II - 1

In the form above, and with the help of Table I - Sun, which shows the benefic position of Sun with reference to itself and 7 other planets including Lagna, mark Bindus in the relevant columns. *Remember that counting would start from asterisk mark in each column. As this is the first position from where counting would begin.* Sun as per Table 1 has benefic Bindus in places 1, 2, 4, 7, 8, 9, 10 and 11 from Saturn. As Saturn is in Cancer the counting would start from this sign it self. First Bindu would be put under sign

Cancer, second Bindu under sign Leo, 3rd under sign Libra as this is in 4th place from Cancer, then under sign Capricorn as this is 7th from Cancer, next under sign Aquarius, next under sign Pisces, next under sign Aries and last under Taurus as it is 11th place from Cancer where Saturn is placed. Now continue with the Sun's position with reference to Jupiter in the next column. Sun with reference to Jupiter is benefic in places 5, 6, 9 and 11. Start counting from asterisk under Taurus where Jupiter is located. 1st Bindu would start from Virgo, 5th from Taurus. Next Bindu would be under sign Libra 6th from Taurus, next under Capricorn and last under Pisces. In similar way continue with other planets, Mars, Sun (itself), Venus, Mercury and Moon. Total Picture that will emerge is as shown in Table II - 1.

Chart 2 - Prastharashtakvarga of Moon Table II - 2

Follow the same procedure as above. Table 1 shows the benefic positions of Moon with respect to itself and other 6 planets and Lagna.

Before planting the Bindus in the chart, make an asterisk mark of all the planets and Lagna, because this is the position from where the counting would start.

Ist column Saturn: Moon is benefic in 3, 5, 6 and 11 places from Saturn. The first Bindu would be in third sign from Cancer where Saturn is located. The second Bindu would be in the 5th from Saturn i.e. Scorpio. The third Bindu would be in the 6th from Saturn i.e. Sagittarius and last would be in the 11th from Saturn i.e. in Taurus.

From Jupiter: First Bindu in first from Taurus where Jupiter is located i.e. in sign Taurus itself, next in 4th from Jupiter i.e. Leo and so on in Scorpio, Sagittarius, Capricorn, Aquarius, Pisces and Aries.

From Mars: Bindus would be in 2, 3, 5, 6, 9, 10 & 11 from Mars or from sign Leo.

From Sun: Bindus would be in 3, 6, 7, 8, 10 & 11 from Scorpio, the position of Sun.

From Venus: Bindus would be in 3, 4, 5, 7, 9, 10 & 11 from sign Sagittarius or sign occupied by Venus.

From Mercury: Bindus would be in 1, 3, 4, 5, 7, 8, 10 & 11 from Scorpio.

From Moon: Bindus would be in 1, 3, 6, 7, 10 & 11 from Moon or sign Capricorn.

From Lagna: Bindus would be in 3, 6, 10 & 11 from Lagna or sign Cancer. This is as shown in Table II-2.

Continue in this manner for rest of planets Mars, Mercury, Jupiter, Venus and Saturn.

This would be as in Charts II - (3, 4, 5, 6 and 7)

Construct rest of the charts for planets Mars, Mercury, Jupiter, Venus and Saturn, as in the charts Table II -3, 4, 5, 6 and 7.

Now total all the figures from Chart II-I to 7 Rashi wise and put in the chart of Sarvashtakvarga as Chart III-

Table A

Rashis / Planets	Aries	Taurus Jupiter	Gemini	Cancer Lag, Sat	Leo Mars	Virgo	Libra	Scorpio Mer, Sun	Sagi. Rah, Ven	Capri. Moon	Aqua.	Pisces	Total
Saturn				*									
Jupiter		*											
Mars					*								
Sun								*					
Venus									*				
Mercury								*					
Moon										*			
Lagna			*										
Total													

Table II-1

Sun's Prastharashtakvarga: Benefic points with reference to places marked *

Rashis / Planets	Aries	Taurus Jupiter	Gemini	Cancer Lag, Sat	Leo Mars	Virgo	Libra	Scorpio Mer, Sun	Sagittarius Venus	Capricorn Moon	Aquarius	Pisces	Total
Saturn 1, 2, 4, 7, 8, 9, 10, 11	0	0		*0	0		0			0	0	0	8
Jupiter 5, 6, 9, 11		*				0	0			0		0	4
Mars 1, 2, 4, 7, 8, 9, 10, 11	0	0	0		0*	0		0			0	0	8
Sun 1, 2, 4, 7, 8, 9, 10, 11		0	0	0	0	0		*0	0		0		8
Venus 6, 7, 12		0	0					0	*				3
Mercury 3, 5, 6, 9, 10, 11, 12	0			0	0	0	0	*		0		0	7
Moon 3, 6, 10, 11			0				0	0		*		0	4
Lagna 3, 4, 6, 10, 11, 12	0	0	0	*			0	0		0			6
Total	**4**	**5**	**5**	**3**	**4**	**5**	**5**	**4**	**2**	**3**	**3**	**5**	**48**

Table II-2

Moon's Prastharashtakvarga: Benefic points with reference to places marked *

Rashis / Planets	Aries	Taurus Jupiter	Gemini	Cancer Lag, Sat	Leo Mars	Virgo	Libra	Scorpio Mer, Sun	Sagittarius Venus	Capricorn Moon	Aquarius	Pisces	Total
Saturn 3, 5, 6, 11		0		*		0		0	0				4
Jupiter 1, 4, 7, 8, 10, 11, 12	0	* 0			0			0	0		0	0	7
Mars 2, 3, 5, 6, 9, 10, 11	0	0	0		*	0	0		0	0			7
Sun 3, 6, 7, 8, 10, 11	0	0	0		0	0		*		0			6
Venus 3, 4, 5, 7, 9, 10, 11	0		0		0	0	0		*		0	0	7
Mercury 1, 3, 4, 5, 7, 8, 10, 11		0	0		0	0		* 0		0	0	0	8
Moon 1, 3, 6, 7, 10, 11			0	0			0	0		0 *		0	6
Lagna 3, 6, 10, 11	0	0		*		0			0				4
Total	5	6	5	1	4	6	3	4	4	4	3	4	49

Table II—3

Mars's Prastharashtakvarga Benefic points with reference to places marked *

Rashis Planets	Aries	Taurus Jupiter	Gemini	Cancer Lag, Sat	Leo Mars	Virgo	Libra	Scorpio Mer, Sun	Sagittarius Venus	Capricorn Moon	Aquarius	Pisces	Total
Saturn 1, 4, 7, 8, 9, 10, 11	0	0		* 0			0			0	0	0	7
Jupiter 6, 10, 11, 12	0	*					0				0	0	4
Mars 1, 2, 4, 7, 8, 10, 11		0	0		* 0	0		0			0	0	7
Sun 3, 5, 6, 10, 11	0				0	0		*		0		0	5
Venus 6, 8, 11, 12		0		0			0	0	*				4
Mercury 3, 5, 6, 11	0					0		*		0		0	4
Moon 3, 6, 11			0					0		*		0	3
Lagna 1, 3, 6, 10, 11	0	0		*0		0			0				5
Total	5	4	2	3	2	4	3	3	1	3	3	6	39

Table II-4

Mercury's Prastharashtakvarga Benefic points with reference to places marked *

Rashis / Planets	Aries	Taurus Jupiter	Gemini	Cancer Lag, Sat	Leo Mars	Virgo	Libra	Scorpio Mer, Sun	Sagittarius Venus	Capricorn Moon	Aquarius	Pisces	Total
Saturn 1, 2, 4, 7, 8, 9, 10, 11	0	0		0*	0		0			0	0	0	8
Jupiter 6, 8, 11, 12	0	*					0		0			0	4
Mars 1, 2, 4, 7, 8, 9, 10, 11	0	0	0		0*	0	0				0	0	8
Sun 5, 6, 9, 11, 12	0				0		0	0	*			0	5
Venus 1, 2, 3, 4, 5, 8, 9, 11	0			0	0		0		0*	0	0	0	8
Mercury 1, 3, 5, 6, 9, 10, 11, 12	0			0	0	0	0	0*		0		0	
Moon 2, 4, 6, 8, 10, 11	0		0		0		0	0		*	0		6
Lagna 1, 2, 4, 6, 9, 10, 11	0	0		0*	0		0		0		0		7
Total	8	3	2	5	6	3	7	3	3	3	5	6	54

Table II 5

Jupiter's Prastharashtakvarga Benefic points with reference to places marked *

Rashis / Planets	Aries	Taurus Jupiter	Gemini	Cancer Lag, Sat	Leo Mars	Virgo	Libra	Scorpio Mer, Sun	Sagittarius Venus	Capricorn Moon	Aquarius	Pisces	Total
Saturn 3, 5, 6, 12			0	*		0		0	0				4
Jupiter 1, 2, 3, 4, 7, 8, 10, 11		0*	0	0	0			0	0		0	0	8
Mars 1, 2, 4, 7, 8, 10, 11		0	0		0*	0		0			0	0	7
Sun 1, 2, 3, 4, 7, 8, 9, 10, 11		0	0	0	0	0		0*	0	0	0		9
Venus 2, 5, 6, 9, 10, 11	0	0			0	0	0		*	0			6
Mercury 1, 2, 4, 5, 6, 9, 10, 11	0			0	0	0		0*	0		0	0	8
Moon 2, 5, 7, 9, 11		0		0		0		0		*	0		5
Lagna 1, 2, 4, 5, 6, 7, 9, 10, 11	0	0		0*	0		0	0	0	0		0	9
Total	3	6	4	5	6	6	2	7	5	3	5	4	56

Table II 6

Venus's Prastharashtakvarga Benefic points with reference to places marked *

Rashis Planets	Aries	Taurus Jupiter	Gemini	Cancer Lag, Sat	Leo Mars	Virgo	Libra	Scorpio Mer, Sun	Sagittarius Venus	Capricorn Moon	Aquarius	Pisces	Total
Saturn 3, 4, 5, 8, 9, 10, 11	0	0		*		0	0	0			0	0	7
Jupiter 5, 8, 9, 10, 11		*				0			0	0	0	0	5
Mars 3, 5, 6, 9, 11, 12	0		0	0	*		0		0	0			6
Sun 8, 11, 12			0			0	0	*					3
Venus 1, 2, 3, 4, 5, 8, 9, 10, 11	0			0	0	0	0		0*	0	0	0	9
Mercury 3, 5, 6, 9, 11	0			0		0		*		0		0	5
Moon 1, 2, 3, 4, 5, 8, 9, 11, 12	0	0			0	0		0	0	0*	0	0	9
Lagna 1, 2, 3, 4, 5, 8, 9, 11		0		0*	0	0	0	0			0	0	8
Total	5	3	2	4	3	7	5	3	4	5	5	6	52

Table II 7

Saturn's Prastharashtakvarga Benefic points with reference to places marked *

Rashis / Planets	Aries	Taurus Jupiter	Gemini	Cancer Lag, Sat	Leo Mars	Virgo	Libra	Scorpio Mer, Sun	Sagittarius Venus	Capricorn Moon	Aquarius	Pisces	Total
Saturn 3, 5, 6, 11		0		*		0		0	0				4
Jupiter 5, 6, 11, 12	0	*				0	0					0	4
Mars 3, 5, 6, 10, 11, 12		0	0	0	*		0		0	0			6
Sun 1, 2, 4, 7, 8, 10, 11		0	0		0	0		0*	0		0		7
Venus 6, 11, 12		0					0	0	*				3
Mercury 6, 8, 9, 10, 11, 12	0		0	0	0	0	0	*					6
Moon 3, 6, 11			0					0		*		0	3
Lagna 1, 3, 4, 6, 10, 11	0	0		*0		0	0		0				6
Total	3	5	4	3	2	5	5	4	4	1	1	2	39

Now total all the Bindus in 12 Rashis.

Table III

Sarvashtakvarga or Samudayashatakvarga

Rashis / Planets	Aries	Taurus Jupiter	Gemini	Cancer Lag, Sat	Leo Mars	Virgo	Libra	Scorpio Mer, Sun	Sagittarius Venus	Capricorn Moon	Aquarius	Pisces	Total
Sun	4	5	5	3	4	5	5	4	2	3	3	5	48
Moon	5	6	5	1	4	6	3	4	4	4	3	4	49
Mars	5	4	2	3	2	4	3	3	1	3	3	6	39
Mercury	8	3	2	5	6	3	7	3	3	3	5	6	54
Jupiter	3	6	4	5	6	6	2	7	5	3	5	4	56
Venus	5	3	2	4	3	7	5	3	4	5	5	6	52
Saturn	3	5	4	3	2	5	5	4	4	1	1	2	39
Total	**33**	**32**	**24**	**24**	**27**	**36**	**30**	**28**	**23**	**22**	**25**	**33**	**337**

Chart III – (Indira Gandhi – Sarvashtakvarga)

33	33	32	24
25	Chart III - 8 Indira Gandhi Sarvashtakvarga Showing benefic bindus		24 Lag
22			27
23	28	30	36

Direct Casting of Sarvashtakvarga Chakra

Make use of the Table S.

It would be observed that Sun with reference to 1st Bhava (place) from itself contributes 3 Bindus; in 2nd, 3rd and 4th also 3 Bindus; in the 5th Bhava 2 Bindus; in 6th 3 Bindus; in 7th 4 Bindus; in 8th Bhava 5 Bindus; in 9th Bhava 3 Bindus; in 10th Bhava 5 Bindus; in 11th 7 and 12th Bhava 2 Bindus. Similarly this chart shows benefic positions with reference to other planets and so on.

Now take a blank chart in the form X-I and put asterisk mark at position of planets as these exist in birth horoscope. This asterisk sign would be starting sign for counting Bindus in each case.

Chart X-II

With the help of Chart - above start filling up the columns with number of Bindus. Remember that counting in each case should start from the asterisk mark i.e. the Rashi where each planet is located in the birth chart.

In the case of Sun which is located in Scorpio the 1st house would be Scorpio itself. Therefore, as per chart above Scorpio would have 3 Bindus, 2nd or Sagittarius would again have 3 Bindus, 3rd or Capricorn 3 Bindus, 4th or Aquarius 3 Bindus, 5th or Pisces 2 Bindus, 6th or Aries 3 Bindus, 7th or Taurus 4 Bindus and so on. Repeat the exercise in case of rest of planets. Moon is located in Capricorn, therefore Capricorn will be the 1st house which gets 2 Bindus, 2nd is Aquarius and gets 3 Bindus, Pisces is 3rd and gets 5 Bindus, Aries is 4th and gets 2 Bindus and so on.

Next Mars is located in Leo, the 1st house would be Leo itself. Therefore, as per chart above Leo would have 3 Bindus, 2nd or Virgo would again have 3 Bindus, 3rd or Scorpio 3 Bindus, 4th or Sagittarius 3 Bindus, 5th or Capricorn 2 Bindus, 6th or Aquarius 3, 7th 4 Bindus and so on. Repeat the exercise in case of rest of planets.

Mercury is located in Scorpio, therefore Scorpio will be the 1st house which gets 3 Bindus, 2nd is Sagittarius and gets 1 Bindu, Capricorn is 3rd and gets 5 Bindus, Aquarius is 4th and gets 2 Bindus and so on.

Jupiter is located in Taurus as such it is the 1st house. This gets as per Table C-X-I,

4 Bindus in the 1st house i.e. in Taurus itself, 2nd or Gemini gets 1 Bindu and so on.

Venus is located in Sagittarius, therefore, Sagittarius becomes the lst house. This gets 2 Bindus. The next house is Capricorn which gets 3 Bindus, 3rd is Aquarius and gets again 3 Bindus and so on.

Saturn is the last planet. Since it is placed in Cancer, this becomes the 1st house and so on.

Total the figures. This will take shape as in Table X-II.

Result from Table III & Table C-X is same with respect to the preparation of Sarvashtakvarga, now we fill up these Bindus in the natal chart.

Important Note: This chart should only be used for arriving at the total. For individual benefic point of each planet (Bhinnashtakvarga) earlier separate charts will have to be made.

Table of Benefic Points

Table S

Places	Ist	2nd	3rd	4th	5th	6th	7th	8th	9th	10th	11th	12th	Total
Sun	3	3	3	3	2	3	4	5	3	5	7	2	43
Moon	2	3	5	2	2	5	2	2	2	3	7	1	36
Mars	4	5	3	4	3	3	4	4	4	6	7	2	49
Mercury	3	1	5	2	6	6	1	2	5	5	7	3	46
Jupiter	2	1	1	2	3	4	2	4	2	4	7	4	36
Venus	2	3	3	3	4	4	2	3	4	3	6	3	40
Saturn	3	2	4	4	4	3	3	4	4	4	6	1	42
Lagna	5	3	5	5	2	6	1	2	2	6	7	1	45
Total													337

Table X-I
Direct Casting of Ashtakvarga without Bhinnashtak

Rashis / Planets	Aries	Taurus Jupiter	Gemini	Cancer Lag, Sat	Leo Mars	Virgo	Libra	Scorpio Mer, Sun	Sagittarius Venus	Capricorn Moon	Aquarius	Pisces	Total
Sun								*					
Moon										*			
Mars					*								
Mer								*					
Jupiter		*											
Venus									*				
Saturn				*									
Lagna				*									
Total													

Counting to start from * sign as this would be first house

Table X-II
Indira Gandhi
Direct Casting of Ashtakvarga without Bhinnashtak

Rashis / Planets	Aries	Taurus Jupiter	Gemini	Cancer Lag, Sat	Leo Mars	Virgo	Libra	Scorpio Mer, Sun	Sagittarius Venus	Capricorn Moon	Aquarius	Pisces	Total
Sun	3	4	5	3	5	7	2	*3	3	3	3	2	43
Moon	2	2	5	2	2	2	3	7	1	*2	3	5	36
Mars	4	6	7	2	*4	5	3	4	3	3	4	4	49
Mer	6	1	2	5	5	7	3	*3	1	5	2	6	46
Jupiter	4	*2	1	1	2	3	4	2	4	2	4	7	36
Venus	4	4	2	3	4	3	6	3	*2	3	3	3	40
Saturn	5	6	1	*3	2	4	4	4	3	3	4	4	42
Lagna	6	7	1	*5	3	5	5	2	6	1	2	2	45
Total	34	32	24	24	27	36	30	28	23	22	25	33	337

Chapter 3

Reductions (Shodhan)

The figures in Bhinnashtakvarga of each planet are subject to two types of reductions. These reductions are made for calculating longevity and making other predictions which will be discussed in later chapters. These are known as:

1. **Trikona Shodhan or 1ˢᵗ Reduction and**

2. **Ekadhipatya Shodhan or 2ⁿᵈ Reduction**

Trikona reduction is carried out first and thereafter Ekadhipatya is applied. This order cannot be reversed.

Trikona Reduction

Twelve Rashis of a horoscope are divided into four trinal types:

1. Fiery   - Aries, Leo and Sagittarius or signs 1, 5 and 9.

2. Earthy   - Taurus, Virgo and Capricorn or signs 2, 6 and 10.

3. Airy   - Gemini, Libra and Aquarius or signs 3, 7 and 11.

4. Watery   - Cancer, Scorpio and Pisces or signs 4, 8 and 12.

Reduction is to be carried out separately in each type.

For Trikona Shodhan

In Trikona Shodhan, Rashis of the same Tatwa i.e. Agni, Prithvi, Vayu and Jal are grouped together i.e. 1, 5, 9; 2, 6, 10; 3, 7, 11; and 4, 8, 12 from Meshadi Rashis. Rashis of the same tatwa represent the trine houses and hence the reduction carried out is called Trikona Shodhan. Trikona Shodhan is performed for a particular purpose in Ashtakvarga because it tells us about one particular tatwa's strength in a horoscope. If any one or two trines are strong, then that Bhava attains immense strength. If for Mesha its trines Simha or Dhanu are strong then all the three Rashis get strength because they fall into the same group. The principles of Trikona Shodhan are as under:

Rules:

1. If the figures in three sign are unequal deduct lowest from all the three and retain the remainder. (This view is that of Parashara and is followed in this book. There is another view among scholars which has been discussed under the chapter controversies on Ashtakvarga.)

2. No reduction is to be carried out if one of the figures in anyone of the three signs is 0.

3. If there are no figures in two of the signs make third also zero i.e. eliminates the third.

4. If figures in all the three signs are equal then eliminate all or make them equal to 0.

Note: There are also other views regarding rule 3. But we are following here the most accepted principles.

Example: Let us take the chart of Bhinnashtak of Sun in the horoscope of Indira Gandhi and make Trikona or 1st Reduction.

Indira Gandhi
Trikona Reduction, A Sun, Table II-1

5	4	5	5
3	Sun's Ashtakvarga before Reduction		3 Lag
3			4
2	4	5	5

1. Signs - Aries, Leo and Sagittarius

Sign	Aries	Leo	Sagittarius
Number of Bindus	4	4	2
Deduct lowest number	-2	-2	-2
Reduced number of Bindus	2	2	0

2. Signs - Taurus, Virgo and Capricorn

Sign	Taurus	Virgo	Capricorn
Number of Bindus	5	5	3
Deduct lowest number	-3	-3	-3
Reduced number of Bindus	2	2	0

3. Signs - Gemini, Libra & Aquarius

Sign	Gemini	Libra	Aquarius
Number of Bindus	5	5	3
Deduct lowest number	-3	-3	-3
Reduced number of Bindus	2	2	0

4. Signs - Cancer, Scorpio and Pisces

Sign	Cancer	Scorpio	Pisces
Number of Bindus	3	4	5
Deduct lowest number	-3	-3	-3
Reduced number of Bindus	0	1	2

2	2	2	2
0	Sun's Ashtakvarga after 1st Reduction		0 Lag
0			2
0	1	2	2

Moon's Ashtakvarga

Table II-2

II Moon's Ashtakvarga

Ist reduction- Trikona reduction

4	5	6	5
3	Moon Ashtakvarga before Reduction		1 Lag
4			4
4	4	3	6

1. Signs - Aries, Leo and Sagittarius

Signs	Aries	Leo	Sagittarius
No. of Bindus	5	4	4
Deduct lowest	-4	-4	-4
Reduced Bindus	1	0	0

2. Signs - Taurus, Virgo and Capricorn

Signs	Taurus	Virgo	Capricorn
Number of Bindus	6	6	4
Deduct lowest Bindus	-4	-4	-4
Reduced Bindus	2	2	0

3. Signs - Gemini, Libra & Aquarius

Signs	Gemini	Libra	Aquarius
Number of Bindus	5	3	3
Deduct lowest Bindus	-3	-3	-3
Reduced Bindus	2	0	0

4. Signs - Cancer, Scorpio and Pisces

Signs	Cancer	Scorpio	Pisces
Number of Bindus	1	4	4
Deduct lowest	-1	-1	-1
	0	3	3

3	1	2	2
0	Moon Ashtakvarga after 1st Reduction		0 Lag
0			0
0	3	0	2

Mars Ashtakvarga, Table II-3

6	5	4	2
3	Mars Ashtakvarga before Reduction		3 Lag
3			2
1	3	3	4

3	4	1	0
1	Mars Ashtakvarga after 1st Reduction		0 Lag
0			1
0	0	1	1

Mercury's Ashtakvarga, Table II-4

6	8	3	2
5	Mercury's Ashtakvarga before Reduction		5 Lag
3			6
3	3	7	3

3	5	0	0
3	Mercury's Ashtakvarga after 1st Reduction		2 Lag
0			3
0	0	5	0

Jupiter's Ashtakvarga, Table II-5

4	3	6	4
5	Jupiter's Ashtakvarga before Reduction		5 Lag
3			6
5	7	2	6

0	0	3	2
3	Jupiter's Ashtakvarga after 1st Reduction		1 Lag
0			3
2	3	0	3

Venus Ashtakvarga, Table II-6

6	5	3	2
5	Venus's Ashtakvarga before Reduction		4 Lag
5			3
4	3	5	7

3	2	0	0
3	Venus's Ashtakvarga after 1st Reduction		1 Lag
2			0
1	0	3	4

Saturn's Ashtakvarga, Table II-7

2	3	5	4
1	Saturn's Ashtakvarga before Reduction		3 Lag
1			2
4	4	5	5

0	1	4	3
0	Saturn's Ashtakvarga after 1st Reduction		1 Lag
0			0
2	2	4	4

2nd or Ekadhipatya reduction

After Trikona reduction has been carried out, the next reduction would be Ekadhipatya reduction or 2nd Reduction.

Rules

1. Ekadhipatya means ownership of two signs by a planet. Sun and Moon own one sign each, Cancer and Leo. Therefore, no reduction is to be carried out in these two Rashis.

2. In other cases five other planets Mars, Mercury, Jupiter, Venus and Saturn own two signs each. In these cases the reduction is to be carried out as follows:

    No reduction is carried out in case there are planets (excluding Rahu and Ketu) in both the Rashis owned by a planet. It means if both signs are occupied no reduction is to be made. For example if in case of Rashis Aries and Scorpio owned by Mars there are planets in both Rashis no reduction is called for. Rahu and Ketu are not taken into consideration as planets for this purpose. Remember the sign with planets becomes strong and is not to be disturbed. On this basis proceed as follows.

3. No reduction is also to be made if one of the signs belonging to same planet has zero figures, whether occupied or not.

4. **If one of the two signs is occupied by** a planet and the other is not, proceed as follows:

    Keeping the figures in sign occupied as they are; there are three different possibilities

    (a)   Figure in the sign not occupied by a planet is more than the sign occupied. In such cases make figures equal to those of occupied one. Remember earlier formula that a sign with a planet is strong and is not to be disturbed.

    (b) & (c) Figures in non - occupied are equal to or less than those of occupied. In such cases remove figures in non - occupied.

5. **Both Signs Unoccupied** - If figures in both the signs which are unoccupied are equal, remove figures in both i.e. make them zero. If figures are unequal; make the larger figure equal to smaller one.

Note: In some books the method of reduction is slightly different. Here we are following the most accepted one.

Now in the light of these observations let us make 2nd or Ekadhipatya reduction in case of Ashtakvarga of Sun in the horoscope of Indira Gandhi. Figures after 1st reduction are as below.

Sun's Ashtakvarga after 1st reduction

Diamond chart (left):

	(2) Mar		(2)	
(2)	5	6	(0) Sat	3	2	(2) Jup
(2)		7	4 1 10		(2)
(1) Sun Mer	8	(0) Mon	9	12 11	(2)
(0) Rah Ven			(0)	

Grid table (right):

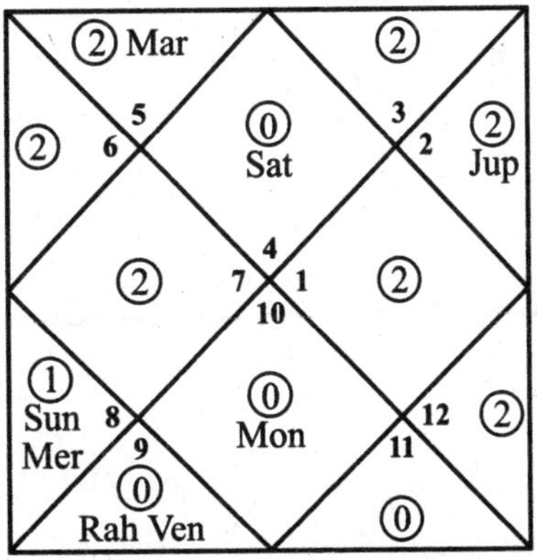

2	2	2 Jup	2
0	Indira Gandhi: Sun's Ashtakavarga After 1st Reduction		0 Lag Sat
0 Mon			2 Mar
0 Rah Ven	1 Sun Mer	2	2

1. Signs Cancer and Leo are not to be disturbed as Sun and Moon are owners of one Rashi. Rule 1.

2. The signs of Mars are Aries and Scorpio. The number of Bindus are 2 in Aries and 1 in Scorpio. Since Scorpio is occupied there is no reduction. Aries has 2 Bindu and unoccupied. So make it equal to occupied one i.e. 1.

3. The signs of Venus are Taurus and Libra. The number of Bindus are 2 in Taurus occupied by Jupiter, so no change, and 2 in Libra unoccupied by any planet, so make it 0. Rule 4.

4. Signs of Mercury are Gemini and Virgo with Bindus 2 and 2 respectively. Both are unoccupied therefore remove figures

from both meaning make them equal to 0. Rule 5.

5.   Signs of Jupiter are Sagittarius and Pisces. Sagittarius has 0 Bindu, while Pisces has 2. Sagittarius is occupied, while Pisces is not. Since one of the signs has 0 figure no change - rule 3 above.

6.   Signs of Saturn, Capricorn and Aquarius. Both the signs have 0 figures, therefore no change.

Chart of Sun's Ashtakvarga after 2nd reduction would be:-

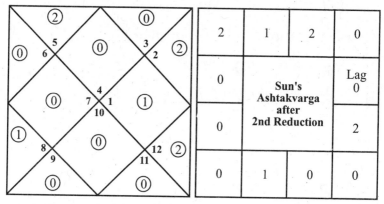

2nd Reduction in Ashtakvarga of Moon in Indira Gandhi's horoscope

Chart showing Moon's Ashtakvarga after 1st reduction is as shown on next page.

1.   Signs Cancer and Leo - No Change - Rule I

2.   Signs of Mars: Aries and Scorpio. Aries have 1 Bindus and is unoccupied. Scorpio is occupied and has 3 Bindu. This is not to be disturbed. The other sign Aries which is non-occupied has less Bindus than the occupied one Scorpio. Therefore make figures 0 in Aries.

3. Signs of Venus: Taurus is occupied and has 2 Bindus as Libra is unoccupied and has 0 Bindu, so no change.

4. Signs of Mercury: Gemini and Virgo One of the signs have 0 figures, therefore no change.

5. Signs of Jupiter: Sagittarius is occupied and Pisces is not. Since one of the signs has no Bindu hence no change.

6. Signs of Saturn: Capricorn and Aquarius. Both are unoccupied, and since one sign has no Bindu, there is no reduction.

3	1	2 Jup	2 Ket
0	Moon's Ashtakvarga after 1st Reduction		0 Lag Sat
0 Mon			0 Mar
0 Rah Ven	3 Sun Mer	0	2

3	0	2	0
0	Moon's Ashtakvarga after 2nd Reduction		0 Lag
0			0
0	3	0	0

Similarly carry out reductions for other planets which would be as on next page:

3	4	1	0
1	Mar's Ashtakvarga after 2nd Reduction		0 Lag
0			1
0	0	0	1

3	5	0	0
3	Mercury's Ashtakvarga after 2nd Reduction		2 Lag
0			3
0	0	5	0

0	0	3	2
3	Jupiter's Ashtakvarga after 2nd Reduction		1 Lag
0			3
2	3	0	2

<table>
<tr><td>0</td><td></td><td>0</td></tr>
</table>

1	2	0	0
2	Venus's Ashtakvarga after 2nd Reduction		1 Lag
2			0
1	0	3	4

0	0	4	3
0	Saturn's Ashtakvarga after 2nd Reduction		1 Lag
0			0
2	2	0	3

Chapter 4

Reduction in Sarvashtakvarga

Mandal Shodhana

The total number of Bindus in each Rashi in **Sarvashtakvarga** undergoes three types of reduction

1	Reduction No 1	Mandal Shodhana
2	Reduction No 2	Trikona Reduction
3.	Reduction No 3	Ekadhipatya Reduction

Total numbers of Bindus are divided by 12 and remainder obtained. If the remainder is 0 make it equal to 12. This is called Mandal Shodhana. i.e. Reduction no. 1.

Example: Horoscope of Indira Gandhi:

Sarvashtakchakra

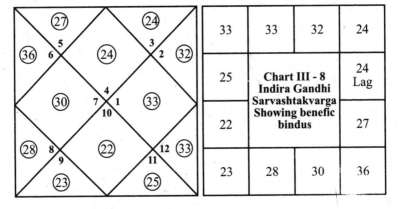

Expunge the multiples of 12.

9	9	8 Jup	12
1	Indira Gandhi After expunging multiples of 12 Mandal Shodhana		12 Lag Sat
10 Mon			3 Mar
11 Rah Ven	4 Sun Mer	6	12

2nd Reduction - Trikona Reduction:

In Sign 1, 5 and 9 deduct lowest figure 3: Net result is in Aries 6, Leo 0 and Sagittarius 8

In signs 2, 6, and 10 deduct lowest figure 8

Balance will be in Taurus 0, In Virgo 4 and in Capricorn 2.

In signs 3, 7 and 11 deduct lowest figure 1 Balance would be Gemini 11, Libra 5 and Aquarius 0. Deduct lowest figure 4 from signs 4, 8 and 12. Result would be Cancer 8, Scorpio 0 and Pisces 5.

Sarvashtakchakra after 2nd reduction

5	6	0	11
0	Chart III - 8 Indira Gandhi after 2nd reduction		8 Lag
2			0
8	0	5	4

3rd Reduction

1. There is no reduction in Cancer and Leo.

2. In signs of Mars Scorpio is occupied and has 0 Bindus. Aries which is non occupied has 6 Bindus. No change as one of the signs has 0.

3. In signs of Mercury, Gemini and Virgo both are unoccupied. Make 11 Bindus in Gemini to 4 and Virgo will remain with 4.

4. In signs of Venus, Taurus is occupied with 0 Bindus. Libra has 5. Hence there is no change.

5. In signs of Jupiter Sagittarius and Pisces, Sagittarius is occupied and has 8 Bindus Keep the figures as it is and eliminate figures in Pisces to 0.

6. In the signs of Saturn, Capricorn is occupied and has 2 Bindus and in unoccupied Aquarius sign has 0, there is no change.

The end position would be as follows:

0	6	0 Jup	4
0	Indira Gandhi After 2nd Reduction		8 Sat
2 Mon			0 Mar
8 Rah Ven	0 Sun Mer	5	4

North Indian chart:
- Top: (0) Mar 5
- (4) 6, (8) Sat, 3 2, (0) Jup
- (5) 7 1 (6), 4, 10
- (0) Sun Mer 8, (2) Mon, 12 11 (0)
- 9, (8) Rah Ven, (0)

The reduced figures are too multiplied by *Graha Gunakara* and *Rashi Gunakara* to get Shodhya Pinda as given in next chapter for prediction of events of each Bhava as well as for calculation of longevity.

Chapter 5

Shodhya Pinda

After two reductions have been carried out in each planet, these are subject to following two types of processors:-

1. Rashi Gunakara or Rashi multiplier and

2. Graha Gunakara

Rashi Gunakara

Each Rashi has a fixed number of units allotted to it. This is constant and cannot be changed. These are Rashi Gunakara units

Rashi	Units	Rashi	Units	Rashi	Units
Aries	7	Leo	10	Sagittarius	9
Taurus	10	Virgo	5	Capricorn	5
Gemini	8	Libra	7	Aquarius	11
Cancer	4	Scorpio	8	Pisces	12

Number of Bindus left in each Rashi after second reduction has to be multiplied by the above fixed units allotted to each Rashi. For example in the horoscope of Indira Gandhi number of Bindus left after second reduction in Aries in the Ashtakvarga of Sun is 1. This has to multiply by 7, Rashi multiplier for Aries to arrive at figure 7. Taurus has 2 Bindus. Multiply this with 10 to arrive at figure 20, Gemini has 0 Bindu. Multiply 0 with 8 to get 0 and so on for all the 12 Rashis in Ashtakvarga of Sun. Add the sum total of all the figures in 12 Rashis as arrived at above. This will be Rashi Gunakara in case of Ashtakvarga of Sun in the horoscope of Indira Gandhi. This has to be repeated in case of Ashtakvarga of all the other planets.

Similarly each planet has a constant planetary Unit which cannot be changed, and Bindus of each after second reduction have to be multiplied with these units. These are the Graha Gunakara units:

Planet	Unit	Planet	Unit	Planet	Unit	Planet	Unit
Sun	5	Mars	8	Jupiter	10	Saturn	5
Moon	5	Mercury	5	Venus	7		

For example in the horoscope of Indira Gandhi in the Ashtakvarga of Sun, Sun is left with 1 Bindu. This has to be multiplied with 5, number of Bindus left with Moon is 0, multiply 0 with 5 to get 0. Mars has 2 Bindus, multiply 2 with 8 to get 16. Mercury has 1 Bindu, multiply 1 with 5 to get 5. Jupiter has 2 Bindus, multiply it with 10 to get 20. Venus has 0 Bindus, multiply it with 7 to get 0. Similarly figures for Saturn would also be 0.

The products of these two have to be added to get Shodhya Pinda of Sun. This has to be repeated in case of Ashtakvarga of all the seven planets.

Example of Indira Gandhi's horoscope

The above process has been simplified in the tabulated form and is given below:

Planet In Rashi	Planets	GunaKar Bal	Sun		Moon		Mars		Merc		Jup		Venus		Saturn		SAV	
			Bindu	Total Value	Bindu	Total Value	Bindu	Total Value	Bindu	Total Value	Bindu	Total Value	Bindu	Total Value	Bindu	Total Value	Bindu	Total Value
8	Sun	5	1	5	3	15	0	0	0	0	3	15	0	0	2	10	0	0
10	Moon	5	0	0	0	0	0	0	0	0	0	0	2	10	0	0	2	10
5	Mars	8	2	16	0	0	1	8	3	24	3	24	0	0	0	0	0	0
8	Merc.	5	1	5	3	15	0	0	0	0	3	15	0	0	2	10	0	0
2	Jup.	10	2	20	2	20	1	10	0	0	3	30	0	0	4	40	0	0
9	Venus	7	0	0	0	0	0	0	0	0	2	14	1	7	2	14	8	56
4	Sat.	5	0	0	0	0	0	0	2	10	1	5	1	5	1	5	8	40
	Total Value of Planets:			46		50		18		34		103		22		79		106

Now multiply the Bindus left in each Rashi after two reductions with Rashi multiplier to get total figures in RASHI GUNAKARA:-

S No	Rashi	Unit value	Sun		Moon		Mars		Merc		Jup		Ven		Sat		S A V	
1	Aries	7	1	7	0	0	4	28	5	35	0	0	2	14	0	0	6	42
2	Taurus	10	2	20	2	20	1	10	0	0	3	30	0	0	4	40	0	0
3	Gemi	8	0	0	0	0	0	0	0	0	2	16	0	0	3	24	4	32
4	Cance	4	0	0	0	0	0	0	2	8	1	4	1	4	1	4	8	32
5	Leo	10	2	20	0	0	1	10	3	30	3	30	0	0	0	0	0	0
6	Virgo	5	0	0	0	0	1	5	0	0	2	10	4	20	3	15	4	20
7	Libra	7	0	0	0	0	0	0	5	35	0	0	3	21	0	0	5	35
8	Scorpi	8	1	8	3	24	0	0	0	0	3	24	0	0	2	16	0	0
9	Sagitt	9	0	0	0	0	0	0	0	0	2	18	1	9	2	18	8	72
10	Capri	5	0	0	0	0	0	0	0	0	0	0	2	10	0	0	2	10
11	Aquar	11	0	0	0	0	1	11	3	33	3	33	2	22	0	0	0	0
12	Pisces	12	2	24	3	36	3	36	3	36	0	0	1	12	0	0	0	0
	Total Rashi Bala			79		80		100		177		165		112		117		243
	Total Graha Bala			46		50		18		34		103		22		79		106
	Grand Total of Shodhya Pinda			125		130		118		211		268		134		196		349

Chapter 6

Interpretation through Ashtakvarga

While giving predictions in Ashtakvarga we have to see the Bindus contributed by the planet as well as Bindus contained in the Rashi. If a planet has more than 5 Bindus and Rashi has more than 28 Bindus, it gives excellent results. In addition normal rules of astrology should be applied. For a planet to give good results it should not be debilitated or combust, be not in 6, 8 or 12. It should not be in *Papkartari Yoga* or afflicted by malefics. Benefics are good in Kendra, Trikona, malefics are good in 3, 6 and 11 houses.

Even if a planet has got only 4 or less than 4 Bindus in any particular Bhava and is also exalted there, he will not give good results. Likewise, if a planet is placed in an inimical sign or debilitated with more than 4 Bindus, it is bound to give good results. We have to see the transiting planet along with a good dasha. The planet being debilitated and having more than 4 Bindus will give best results. Transit is generally speculative.

If Saturn transit over the sign where Sun, etc. in their Bhinnashtakvarga possesses 0 benefic Bindus, then it will cause diseases, death or death like situation, accidents, loss, fire, etc. according to the planet's natural Karakatwas. Since Sun represents body, transit of Saturn over a *Rashi* where Sun in Bhinnashtak Varga has given 0 points gives bodily problems. If Sun has 0 Bindus in the Bhava where he is placed and also 9th from his Bhava has 0 points, whenever Saturn transits over this 9th house, the native's father will have worries, loss of health, death if a malefic dasha is running. In the Bhinnashtakvarga of Moon, when Saturn transits through a Rashi where Moon has 0 Bindus, it could mean problems to mother; if Mars it will concern brothers or co-born; if Mercury, problems to uncles or relatives; if Jupiter, it will concern children; if Venus, it will be spouse; and if Saturn it will be self. Saturn represents self and *poorva* karmas. Saturn is exalted in Libra (a sign or balance), he is known for justice and will definitely deliver what one deserves. In case Jupiter transits over it one may recover from illness.

For analysing the strength of any house, the Konas should be seen. If Konas are weak the results will not be favourable. Then comes the Karaka, which should also be strong; then we come to the lord of that house. Thereafter, we analyse the dispositor of that house lord. Though one may not own a vehicle yet they have vahana - Sukha. For this we see the 6H and 10H from Venus, which might be having more Bindus. This will give vehicular enjoyments. This above principle can be applied for longevity also. We see the 8H for longevity, 7H for death and 2H for inflicting death or death like situations. While death cannot be avoided, death-like situations can be rightly handled, causing minimum loss.

A planet is strong if it has more than 5 Bindus in its own Bhinnashtakvarga and gives good results in proportion to the greater number of Bindus it has. The planets like Sun, Moon or Mars with 6, 7 or 8 Bindus will confer a high rank on an individual

Signification or *Karkatwa* of planets is important. Briefly significations of planets are:

1. **Sun**: father, condition of health, spiritual maturity high rank and influence in society.

2. **Moon**: mother, intelligence, popularity, condition of mind.

3. **Mars**: Lands, houses, younger co-born, high rank, energy, and sexual prowess.

4. **Mercury**: Speech, intellect, ability to comprehend, level of education etc.

5. **Jupiter**: Wisdom, wealth, children, fame, knowledge of higher

levels, high status.

6. **Venus**: Married life, good looks, perfumes, conveyances, love, art, beauty, etc.

7. **Saturn**: hard work and concentration of mind, longevity, causes of sorrow and sufferings, land and influence over masses.

In interpreting the houses, the normal rules of astrology would apply *e.g.* Bhava flourishes if it contains its own lord or is aspected by it, and also if benefic planets influence it by aspect or position. Strength of the lords of houses is also important.

All planets are weak if they contain 0 to 3 Bindus

With 4 Bindus it is of average strength

With 5 to 8 Bindus, a planet is strong.

Sun

A strong Sun in a horoscope assures high status, excellent health, great respect in society, spiritual maturity, general prosperity and wealth etc.

While a weak Sun having 1 to 4 Bindus gives proneness to diseases, greedy and quarrelsome nature, pessimism and a low status.

Please note that in addition to having large number of Bindus, if a planet is exalted, in its own /friendly house and is aspected by benefics it would give excellent results.

Moon

With more than 5 Bindus it confers high status, wealth, intelligence, prosperity, happy, romantic and kind dispositions with good fortune and long life to mother. Less than 3 Bindus and weak Moon gives dark and dull mind, melancholia and pessimistic mind. Mother also suffers. Moon in Kendra associated with 6 to 8 Bindus makes a person very intelligent, rich and prosperous.

Mars

Strong Mars bestows high status, lands and property, prosperity, leadership and courage. These results are augmented if Mars is exalted or is in its own sign and is placed in a Kendra or Trikona. An exalted Mars or in its own house and placed in 1st, 4th, 9th and 10th house with 7 or 8 Bindus is capable of bestowing great riches, prosperity and high rank.

Mercury

With Mercury having 5 Bindus and placed in a Kendra or Trikona with aspects of Jupiter or Saturn, the person becomes highly learned and powerful speaker.

Weak Mercury in the horoscope gives loss of wealth, lack of intelligence and unhappy relations with family members and friends. With Mercury having 1 to 3 Bindus in 6th or 8th without any benefic aspects the person becomes unreliable and crooked in behavior.

Jupiter

Strong Jupiter gives wisdom, wealth, fortune, high status and optimism, is good for children and pursuit of higher things of life.

With weak Jupiter life becomes unfortunate and full of struggles without wealth, status and learning.

Venus

Strong Venus gives wealth, women and vehicles, pleasures of life, artistic ability.

Weak Venus causes marital problems, poverty, scandals and life without meaning.

Saturn

Strong Saturn is necessary for hard work, concentration of mind, austere life, integrity, deep researches and life of spiritualism.

Weak Saturn causes hindrances, delays, sickness, death, disease and poverty.

Chapter 7

Interpretation through Sarvashtakvarga

Sarvashtakvarga or total number of Bindus is a guide to show the strength of each Bhava. This strength is necessary to know the result of transit in a Bhava. When a planet is transiting in a strong Bhava it gives good results otherwise its capacity to bestow beneficial results is limited. The total number of benefic points in all the twelve Bhavas is 337. Therefore, each Bhava should have an average of 28 points (dividing 337 by 12). If any Bhava has less than 28 points it is considered weak and transit of planet in the weak Rashis gives evil results. Less the number of Bindus weaker is the house.

Please remember that total numbers of benefic and malefic points (*Rekhas*) in a Bhava are 56. If we deduct number of Bindus from 56 we get the number of *Rekhas* in a Bhava. Thus if a Bhava has more than 28 Bindus it is obvious it has less number of Rekhas. If the number of *Rekhas* becomes more then that Bhava becomes weak and gives evil results.

These rules should be interpreted in the light of observations of classical book Prashna Marga which allots minimum number of Bindus for each Bhava and below that Bhava becomes weak as given in the table.

Lagna or 1st house	25	5th House	25	9th House	29
2nd House	22	6th House	34	10th House	36
3rd House	29	7th House	19	11th House	54
4th House	24	8th House	24	12th House	16

Let us see the example of horoscope of Independent India (15, August 1947 time 00:01 hrs midnight).

35	30	44 Lag	19
29	Independent India 14/15.08.1947 Sarvashtakvarga		27
20			27
28	23	25	30

The Lagna of India has 44 Bindus and hence very strong. That is one reason India has survived crisis after crisis. India's weak Rashis are Gemini and Capricorn. The transit of heavy planets Jupiter and Saturn are generally not good as KN Rao has shown in his articles 'Dots of Destiny' published in Astrological Magazine.

⌐It has been stated in classical texts that a house having more than 44 Bindus gives excellent results while with less than 14 Bindus house loses its significance. House with 28 points gives average results.⌐

In addition to seeing the number of Bindus in a house one must also apply normal astrological principles. The house thrives if it is aspected by its own lord, has benefic aspects and has a strong lord. Its Karka should also be well placed.

If Lagna has less Bindus person is sick and has no happiness. , less Bindus in second house mean no wealth, less Bindus in the third make one weak, 4th lack of happiness, 5th no intellect and wicked mind, 6th prone to disease and overpowered by enemies, 7th wrecked married life, 8th long life, 9th sinful, 10th no honour, self respect or employment, 11th house poor, 12th house less expenditure.

Following rules can be applied to Sarvashtakvarga:

1. It follows that it is better if 6th, 8th and 12th houses if they have less Bindus than the Lagna.

2. When planets transits through a strong Rashi it gives good results and in weak Rashi it gives evil results.

3. This has to be modified in the light of normal astrological rules. A planet in its own house or house of exaltation gives good results etc.

4. Houses having Bindus between 25 to 30 are neither strong nor weak.

5. If 11th house has more Bindus than the 10th house then native has to do less struggle to get more gains. He achieves his objectives easily. If 10th house has more Bindus than the 11th house then it means that one has to do more struggles but gets less rewards or he gets opportunity but cannot avail it.

6. When the 10th house has more than 36 Bindus and has no connection with malefic planets one will lead a happy life with wealth earned by his own efforts

7. For illness of self, Bindus of 8th lord from Lagna and 8th lord from Sun in Sarvashtakvarga is to be taken. Add them together and divide by *Janma* Nakshatra. Add the remainder to Bindus 8th from Lagna and subtract by 27. Get the remainder and add the number to the *Janma Nakshatra*. Transit of benefics, especially Jupiter through this Nakshatra will show recovery from illness. For *Mantra Siddhi* or achievement in regard to spiritualism 5th from Lagna and 9th from Sun is taken. Working out in the same way, transit of Jupiter through that Rashi or Nakshatra could indicate success in this regard.

8. **Promotion in Service:**

In the Sarvashtakvarga add Bindus of 10th and 6th house from Lagna. Divide the sum by the number of the *Janma* Nakshatra then add the remainder to the Bindus in the 10th house from Lagna. Subtract by 27. Count from *Janma* Nakshatra so many Nakshatras. Transit of Sun or the 10 lord through this Nakshatra will bring gains in service.

9. **Rules: According to KN Rao** "For career prospects 10th and 11th houses from Lagna, the Sun, *Pada* Lagna and *Karkamsa* must be seen- the 10th house for the nature of such rise and the 11th for the extent of rise

(a) See the benefic points from Lagna in the 10th and 11th houses. If the 11th house has more points the rise will be greater: the greater the difference the higher the rise.

(b) If the 10th house is quite strong (28 or more) but the 11th weak at some stage there is stagnation in one's career.

(c) A very weak 10th house should not be predicted as bad if 11th house is strong enough as it will lift the native.

(d) Correlate all this to major period results.

Variation

Saturn being the significator for profession applies all these rules by judging the 10th and 11th from Saturn. In the case of politicians it is a must. In the case of bureaucrats having political godfathers, it is absolutely necessary.

10th and 11th from Sun: in case of persons who belong to bureaucratic setup with father and in laws in high administrative positions and in right places to lift see Sanjay Gandhi's horoscope.

Case of N. T. Rama Rao

Chart 1 (South Indian & North Indian style birth chart):

	Ven	Sun Mer	Mar
Ket	N.T. Ramarao 12-05-1923 16.43.00 Gudivada, AP		
			Rah
		Lag Mon Jup	Sat

North Indian style chart positions:
- Sat (top), 6/5 Rah
- Mon Jup, 8/9
- 7, 10/4, 1
- Ket 11/12, Ven, 3 Mar
- 2, Sun Mer

Sarvashtakvarga charts:

41	23	23	21
30	N.T. Rama Rao Sarvashtakvarga		35
28			34
30	22	Lag 25	25

North Indian style Sarvashtakvarga:
- (22) (25)
- (30), 8/9, (25), 6/5, (34)
- (28), 7, 10/4, 1, (35)
- (30), 11/12, (23), 3/2, (21)
- (41) (23)

Bindus from Lagna in 10th house 35 and in 11th 34.

Bindus from Saturn in 10th house 21 and in 11th 35.

From Saturn 10th house gets lifted by a strong 11th house.

His 6th house with 41 Bindus gives him strength to fight.

10. If 12th house has more points than 11th house it may mean (i) person has more expenses than earning, which might involve taking loans etc. or (ii) person is earning from foreign sources or country or working in a multi-nation company. A native goes out of country only if his 4th house and its lord is afflicted and has connection with 12th house or its lord.

11. Add the Bindus in the 1st, 4th, 5th, 7th, 9th and 10th houses. This group is called inner self. The second group consists of houses 2, 3, 6, 8, 11 and 12 and is known as outer self whose Bindus should also be added then ascertain which group has more points, if inner self has more Bindus then the native will make money and become wealthy by his own good deeds, learning and knowledge and will be charitable. If outer self is stronger then native is greedy, deceitful, worried man and is a cheat or has to do more struggle to achieve his goal.

12. The twelve houses of the horoscope are divided in four groups or **'Khandas'**. These are:

Bandhu	1st	5th	9th
Sevak	2nd	6th	10th
Poshak	3rd	7th	11th
Ghatak	4th	8th	12th

Add figures in each group. If total in Bandhu is higher than the other groups then the person has independent means of livelihood. He will be rich and charitable and may set up his own business. With 88 or more Bindus one becomes successful businessman

If Sevak total is more than the other groups then the person will be subservient to others.

If Poshak figures are higher than the other groups then the person would be wealthy.

Ghatak figures should never be more than 73. With 80 and above one is never free from enemies, and debts. He is showy and has no family happiness.

A Planet with more than 5 Bindus in its Dasha, Antar, or Gochar gives excellent results.

13. **Period for Prosperity:**

Horoscope has been divided into three sections (based on the analogy whether life is *Alapayu, Madhyaayu* or *Poorna Ayu*).

1. Pisces to Gemini - Period of childhood

2. Cancer to Libra - Youth

3. Scorpio to Aquarius - Old age.

Add figures in each section. The section which has **higher** number of Bindus is the period when a person gets more prosperity.

If there is not much difference in Bindus in the different periods, life runs smooth.

According to some scholars the sections of life start from Lagna as such

      i)   Lagna to 4th house represent childhood

      ii)   5th to 8th house represent Youth

      iii) 9th to 12th house represent old age

While interpreting the horoscope it should also be seen which section of life has more benefic planets as also benefic Bindus. Period with more benefic planets is happier one.

According to P. S. Sastri

1) Add the points of 1 + 4 + 7 + 10 houses. It is called childhood.

2) Add the points of 2 + 5 + 8 +11 houses. It is called young age.

3) Add the points of 3+6+9+12 houses. It is called old age

That period of life will be happy which has more points.

14. **Directions of Prosperity:**

The directions represented by various signs are

Aries, Leo and Sagittarius	East
Taurus, Virgo and Capricorn	South
Gemini, Libra and Aquarius	West
Cancer, Scorpio and Pisces	North

Total the Bindus in 4 different sets of signs. The prosperity will come from the direction which has the highest number of Bindus as also the greater number of benefic planets. It will be useful to work in that direction where maximum numbers of Bindus are located.

Some books use houses in place of Rashis for ascertaining direction.

1)   Add the points of 1+5+9 houses. It is called East direction

2)   Add the points of 2+6+10 houses. It is called South direction

3)   Add the points of 3+7+11 houses. It is called West direction

4)   Add the points of 4+8+12 houses. It is called North direction

5)   In the Sarvashtakvarga if 5th and 9th from Lagna or Sun has less Bindus, and then it is also considered to be an *Arishta* to one's father. Transit of Rahu and Saturn here is not good for father. If Mercury joins this combination it may mean paralysis since Mercury deals with veins. Transit of retrograde planet may prove fatal.

15. Quantum Jump:

It is better if there is not much variation in number of Bindus from one house to other. Much fluctuations show up and down in career and fate, while even distribution of Bindus shows life is running smooth.

Classical case is that of Rajiv Gandhi in whose horoscope 11th house has 50 Bindus as against 10th house with 31 Bindus. He had a meteoric rise and a sudden fall.

If Lagna, 10th and 11th houses have 30 points or more than that native will rise at the age of 37 years of age.

16.   **Period of Sorrow and Agony:**

1.   Total the number of Bindus from Lagna to the sign occupied by Saturn. Multiply the total by 7 and divide it by 27. The Quotient represents the age which may bring sorrow in some form.

2.   Sometimes the counting is done from the sign occupied by Saturn to Lagna – both signs included with above method to follow.

3.   Instead of counting upto Saturn sometime counting is done from Lagna to other malefics, Mars and Rahu or from Mars, Rahu to Lagna.

4.   There is another way of calculation of period of agony. It is total the Bindus from Lagna to sign occupied by Saturn, as also upto sign occupied by Mars and Rahu. Multiply the figures individually by 7 and divide by 27. The remainder gives you a Nakshatra, the transit of malefics over which or over whose trines could cause worry or sorrow.

Period of Happiness:

Similar types of calculations may be done in case of benefics, Jupiter and Venus to arrive at period of happiness.

Combinations for Raj Yogas:

1.   Mars and Venus in exaltation sign, Saturn and Jupiter in Trikona house and Lagna having 40 or more than 40 Bindus.

2.   If Lagna, Moon Lagna and Sun Lagna have 30 points then native will rise by his own efforts.

3.   If Sun and Jupiter are in exaltation sign with 30 points and Lagna has more points than others houses then native will live like a king.

4.   4th and 11th houses have 30 points each then native will prosper at the age of 40 years.

5.   If Lagna, Moon sign, 10th and 11th houses have 30 points each and Jupiter aspect Lagna or Moon, native lives like a king.

6.   Mars and Venus exalted, Saturn in Aquarius and Jupiter having 40 Bindus in Sagittarius in Lagna.

7.   Sun is exalted in Lagna and Jupiter with 40 Bindus is in 4th house.

8.   If malefic planet Saturn, Rahu or Mars is placed in 8th house. The corresponding number of the Sarvashtakvarga will be the age, when native will have bad time.

9.   Same way if benefices are placed in Kendra or Trikona, the corresponding number of Sarvashtakvarga will be the year of age when native will have good times.

10. Moon sign of the couple should have more than 28 point in each other horoscope to have happy married life.

11. Lagna is self, 7th house is partner - Note down the Bindus in Lagna and the 7th house and see which one is stronger. Stronger of the two will control the partner.

According to classical book Maan Saagri if any house has following Bindus the corresponding results given by Bhava and planets occupying etc. would be as under

14 points	Painful, fear of death.
15 points	Fear from Govt.
16 points	Misery.

17 points	Disease or loss of place
18 points	Loss of money
19 points	Quarrelsome and troubles from relatives.
20 points	More expenditure, doing sinful acts.
21 points	Disease, loss of money
22 points	Loss of intellect or memory, weakness and troubles from relatives.
23 points	Worries, pains, loss.
24 points	Loss of money all of sudden or over expenditure.
25 points	Misfortune.
26 points	Troublesome, dullness, fickle nature.
27 points	Over expenditure, worry, anxiety and unclear mind.
28 points	Gain of money but still not satisfied.
29 points	the native receives respect.
30 points	Auspicious results, honour and gain of wealth.
31 to 33 points	good deeds, respects and honour.
34 to 40 points	Native gets all materials prosperity.
41 points	great wealth and many sources of income.
42 points	Materials prosperity, charitable, wealthy, commands love and respect.
43 points	Wealth and happiness
44 to 45 points	Gains of wealth from many sources, receives honours and respects.
46 to 47 points	Native has all best qualities, doing auspicious work.

If 48 and above points: Native has best qualities like a ruler, shows kindness to all, attached to Dharma etc.

While we are analyzing any house we must also see the strength of lord of that house in natural zodiac and Bindus contributed by him to the same number of houses from it. Bhinnashtakvarga of a planet is useful in knowing the strength of the planet and the Bhava he owns. For example in horoscope with Virgo Lagna Jupiter is lord of four and seven Bhava. Then in this horoscope Jupiter will be contributing to both these houses in terms of his Bhinnashtakvarga table. Also for Kaala Purusha Jupiter owns houses 9 and 12. Here Jupiter will always remain permanently Karka for 9 and 12 house. So whenever we are analyzing the strength of 9th Bhava we will invariably see the strength of Jupiter and 9th from Jupiter in Ashtakvarga. Similarly for analyzing 6th Bhavas we will see the 6th house and the contribution made by lord of 6 in this house. In addition we will see sign Virgo and 6th lord from Mercury also as later in natural zodiac is lord of 3 and 6. Thus for analyzing Lagna we will not only see lagan of the horoscope but also Aries sign and Mars its lord.

Predictions through Sarvashtakchakra: Which Part of Life is going to be Happy:

Life is divided into four Ashrams I) Brahmcharya, ii) Grahstya iii) Vanaprashta and iv) Sanyas.

Houses 1st to 4 represent early life, Houses 4 to 7 youth. Houses 7 to 10 middle age and house 10 to 12 old age. Whichever segment has more Bindus that represent the happier period than the other. There is another school of thought who divide the life into three segments, 1 to 33 years on the analogy of Alapayu, 33 to 66 Madhyaayu and 66 to 100 Poorna Ayu. Counting is done from 1st to 4 houses, then from 5th to 8th and last 9 to 12. Whichever segment has more benefic points that period of life is happier one. It is believed that segment 9 to 12 is the best for enjoyment of both wealth as well as spiritual merit. It is better if this segment has more Bindus than the other two. It is believed that Dhan, Dharam and Punya falls into this category which contain both *Vanaprastha* as well as *Sanyas Ashram*. If this segment has more Bindus than the rest life flows easy.

Other Miscellaneous Rules:

In Sarvashtakvarga Lagna should always be stronger than 12, 8 or 6 houses.

11th should have more Bindus than 12th otherwise expenditure will be more than earning.

11th should be equal or more than 2nd. They should not be equal as 11th house is of gains and 2nd of accumulated wealth. If they are equal wealth sustaining capacity is not there.

11th house should be stronger than 6th house otherwise wealth is taken away by enemies.

Normally a Bhava is considered weak if it has less than 28 Bindus but if it has less than 23 Bindus it loses its strength completely. Also for any Bhava to have sustaining capacity, its *Trikona* lords should be having equal if not more strength.

The Bindus in the 11th house should be more than those of 3rd and sixth house otherwise money is taken away by relatives or other people. Hence strength of 11 houses is very important.

10th house should always be strong but should not be stronger than 11th house. However, according to Venkatesha, 10th house should be the strongest since it is the strongest Kendra and represents our Karma which should never fall otherwise our actions and decisions will not be up to mark.

10th house should be stronger in comparison to 8th house which deals with momentary pleasures, secret dealings, immoralities committed on the spur of the moment.

For longevity of a person Bindus in the 8th house are seen which should be less than Lagna Bhava. 7th house Bindus should also be less than Lagna Bhava otherwise it will be a painful or diseased life. One could also be a henpecked husband or his wife could be in a better position than him. Also he may have *Alpayu* if the difference is glaring. If Lagna is life then 7th house represents death; death may overcome life during a malefic dasha - Antardasha.

For services, 6th should not be more than 10th house. If so, one will always be serving others, or may lack decisiveness and qualities of leadership.

Fifth house represents *Poorva Punya Karmas*. It should not have less than 33 Bindus. It should be stronger than Lagna Bhava or at least equal to it but more than 3rd, 6th or 8th house. When 5th and 12th houses have the same number of Bindus, spiritual progress is fast

Fourth house should not have less Bindus than Lagna, 10th or even 9th house. This is because we should be able to enjoy the fruits of karma and *Bhagya*. For materialistic enjoyments 4th Bhava should be equal to 2nd house. To be able to enjoy one's earning 4th Bhava should be stronger than 11th Bhava. In this way one will be helpful to elders also.

Third house is seen for vigour, vitality and courage. If strong, the native will have a forceful personality and may even become a politician or a good sportsperson.

Second house should be stronger than 12th, 6th and 8th houses. If second house is stronger than 7th house, it may indicate multiple marriages. For marital happiness, 2nd house should have lesser Bindus than 7th house.

For vehicles, see the Sarvashtakvarga Bindus in 4th house. Then also see the Trikonas from it, 8th and the 12th houses. If there are more Bindus and position of Venus is also strong one has many conveyances.

In Sarvashtakvarga a Bhava may have good number of points say 31 and a planet may contribute 0 to that Bhava (which is a very rare occurrence or a unique one, since for a Bhava to have good strength in Sarvashtakvarga, each planet should have contributed atleast 1 or 2 points). If it is a malefic Bhava or planet, it is good. We do not see from Lagna Bhava for all aspects of life. If the 5th from any planet (Karaka-wise also) is not good then remedial measures may have to be performed. Poorva Punya is essential for Sukha in life and also the 9th should be good to see if there is Bhagya to enjoy these Poorva Punya Balas. If there is zero in one, the total may not be more than 27 in all, which is generally not possible. Only when Neechabhanga Raj Yoga is found in a horoscope such deviations as contribution by 3 or 4 planets being maximum and others giving minimum or no Bindus at all could take place. This is the reason why Neechabhanga Raj Yoga either lifts a person to great heights or brings him down suddenly.

Chapter 8

Predictions through Ashtakvarga of Sun

According to classical books the transit of Sun over Bhavas with various Bindus gives following results:

0. Bindu	Death or great suffering.
1. Bindu	Worries, sickness, sorrow
2. Bindu	Loss of wealth, theft, quarrel with government
3. Bindu	Aimless travel, mental disturbance
4. Bindu	Mixed results, neither good, nor bad.
5. Bindu	High learning, meeting pious people
6. Bindu	Wealth, high rank, imposing personality.
7. Bindu	High post, commands respect.
8. Bindu	Minister, high dignitary, great honours

Similar results are given for other planets also. These should not be translated literary. Basic rules of Astrology should also be observed. For a planet to be able to give results it should be strong i.e. it should be exalted, in its own house, in *Shubhkartari Yoga*, strong in Vargas, aspected by benefics having more than 5 Bindus in Ashtakvarga, etc.

1. **Sun** with less than 4 Bindus in its Bhinnashtakvarga is supposed to be weak and give adverse results. It has, however been observed, that these Bindus should be less than three and Sun should be weak meaning debilitated, in enemy signs, afflicted by malefics, in Papkartari Yoga, in 6, 8 and 12 only then it gives adverse results.

2. **Sun** with more Bindus in Lagna and well- placed, like in its own house exalted, etc. gives good personality and health. With more than six Bindus it makes a person a born leader.

3. Sun in Lagna, sign of debilitation, or 2 or 10 with only 3 or less Bindus give problems of the heart like heart attack, etc. in Suns Antra and Dasha of lord of the house or of the Navamsa lord of Sun / Lagna Navamsa / planet in Sun's Navamsa.

4. Sun in 10th house gets directional strength. If in addition to its being strong it has more than 5 Bindus it gives a Rajyoga.

5. A strong Sun in the 5th with good number of Bindus makes a person a minister or an ambassador. Weak Sun here is not good for children

6. Sun in the 3rd, 6th, 10th and 11th houses gives excellent results if it is not afflicted. Remember these are Upchahaaya houses or houses of growth.

7. If Sun is in Kendra or Trikona or in 2 house with more than 5 Bindus conjoined or aspected by Mars or Rahu in Rashi or Navamsa, native or his father is likely to die by fire, accident or fall from height.

8. If the Child birth takes place in last quarter of Ashlesha or 1st quarter of Moola and Sun occupies 1st or 5th house with one or 2 Bindus, father dies.

    If the child birth is in 2nd, or 3rd quarter of Revati or Ashwini or last quarter of Ashlesha or Jyeshta child may not meet father in a normal way.

9. While transiting a *Kakshaya* having no Bindus in the Ashtakvarga of Sun it will cause mental tension, misery, sickness and displeasure from the government.

10. Health of a person will be bad if there is a weak Sun in Lagna having less than 3 Bindus.

11. It has been states in classical books that Sun with more than 5

Bindus is not good for father's longevity if it is placed in Kendras or Trikona. (This is not always true. Provided Sun is not afflicted, if it is in its own house or house of a friend in Kendras or Trikonas is always an asset to father.)

I2   In the Bhinnashtakvarga of Sun, Bindus in Lagna or Moon sign should not be less otherwise it is not good for father.

13. In the natal chart, if Sun is conjoined with 3 or more planets, i.e. Mercury, Saturn, Jupiter and has got more than 5 benefic Bindus it gives excellent results.

14. New ventures should not be entered into when Sun transits over a Rashi where it has contributed no Bindus.

15. Add Bindus in trines Aries, Leo and Sagittarius; Taurus, Virgo and Capricorn; Gemini, Libra or Aquarius and Cancer Scorpio and Pisces in Sun Bhinnashtakvarga. Find out which trine is the strongest and the planet contributing maximum Bindus. According to *Vaastu Shashtra*, the prayer room should be located in the direction of the strongest planet.

16. If Sun is placed in the 2nd or the 5th from Lagna and has got less than 3 Bindus, one's father will have early death. We take 2nd and 5th Bhavas because 2nd is a Maraka house and 5th is the Bhavat-Bhava of 9th i.e. 9th from 9H indicating father. 2H is also the 6th from 9H indicating diseases for father.

17. In Sun's Bhinnashtakvarga count the number of Bindus in the 10H from Lagna and also 9th from Sun. Add both. Counting from Ashwini or its trine Nakshatra, when Saturn transits in this Nakshatra, the native's father may die, only if Dasha/ Antardasha is also showing.

Profession from Sun: Sun represents Government, medicine, gold etc. Add the total of fiery signs i.e. 1, 5, 9 in Bhinnashtakvarga of Sun. Multiply by the number of Bindus in Bhinnashtakvarga where Sun is located. Divide both by 12 (or 8 since there are 8 Bindus contributed by planets and Lagna). If the total is equal to or more than 10th Bhava from

Sun then one will have government related job.

From Mars if the product is more than or equal to 10th Bhava in Sun's Bhinnashtakvarga, one will become a Doctor/ Surgeon. In Sun's Bhinnashtakvarga see Sun's contribution in 4th Bhava from Sun or Lagna. If the contribution of Sun is 5 or more than 5 one will have inclination towards medical studies. In Sun's Bhinnashtakvarga, where Mercury is placed is 5 or more than 5, the native will be hard working. Where Mars is placed if the contribution is 5 or more in Sun's Bhinnashtakvarga, the native will become a doctor or will do related work. (Again sometimes the results may not be accurate)

Sun and Death of Father:

1. Use of Shodhya Pinda: (Transit of Saturn)

Multiply the Shodhya Pinda of Sun with figures in the 9th from Sun in the Ashtakvarga of Sun before reduction. Divide the product by 27 and get the remainder. This remainder counted from Ashwini or from the Nakshatra where Saturn is located, the transit of Saturn over which or its trines could prove fatal for father.

Example Horoscope of Indira Gandhi:

Her father JL Nehru died on 27 May 1964. Saturn was in Satabhisha Nakshatra at the time of death

Shodhya Pinda of Sun - 125 x 3 = 375

375 -:- 27 = 24 (Remainder) – 24 from Ashwini is Satabhisha Nakshatra

2. Use of Shodhya Pinda: (Transit of Jupiter)

Multiply the Shodhya Pinda of Sun with figures in the 7th from Jupiter in the Ashtakvarga of Sun before reduction. Divide the product by 27 and get the remainder This remainder counted from Ashwini or from the Nakshatra where Jupiter is located, the transit of Jupiter over which or over whose trines could prove fatal for father

3. Use of Shodhya Pinda: (Transit of Sun)

Multiply the Shodhya Pinda of Sun with figures in the 7th from Sun in the Ashtakvarga of Sun before reduction. Divide the product by 27 and get the remainder. This remainder counted from Ashwini or from the Nakshatra where Sun is located, the transit of Sun over which or its trines could prove fatal for father.

Example:
When Nehru died Sun was in Rohini Nakshatra
SP of Sun = 125
Bindus in 7 from Sun = 5   125 x 5 = 625
625 -:- 27 Remainder = 4
4th Nakshatra from Ashwini is Rohini in Taurus.

One's own death:

Indira Gandhi died on 31 October, 1984. Saturn was in Vishakha Nakshatra no 16

Multiply the Shodhya Pinda of Sun with figures in the 8th from Sun in the Ashtakvarga of Sun before reduction. Divide the product by 27 and get the remainder. This remainder is the Nakshatra the transit of Sun / Saturn over whom or over its trines may prove fatal.

Death of Father without use of Shodhya Pinda:

Take the total number of Bindus in the Ashtakvarga of Sun before both reductions. Multiply this by the figure in the 9th from Sun before reduction and divide the product by 27. The remainder when counted from Ashwini gives you a star the transit of Saturn over which may prove fatal.

Example:

Total number of Bindus in Ashtakvarga of Sun after reduction = 8

Figures in the 9th from Sun before reduction = 3

3x8 = 24 : Satabhisha Nakshatra- Saturn was transiting in Satabhisha at the time of death.

Take the Shodhya Pinda of Sun. Multiply the Bindus in the 9th sign from Sun in Sun's Ashtakvarga before reduction. Divide the product by 12. Get the remainder which counted from Aries gives a sign the transit of Jupiter/ Sun over which proves fatal for father.

Chapter 9

Ashtakvarga of Moon

Moon with 4 Bindus in a horoscope is considered as giving average results, more towards beneficial side.

But if it has 5 to 8 Bindus, then being a royal planet if confers high status, wealth, prosperity, happy attitude of mind with great influence in society, romantic and kind dispositions with good fortune and long life to mother

If it has 0 to 3 Bindus then the person concerned has dark and dull mind, suffers from neuroticism, melancholia and pessimistic mind. Mother of the person will also suffer accordingly.

1. Moon in Kendra associated with 6 to 8 Bindus makes a person very intelligent, rich and prosperous.

2. If Moon is in 6, 8, or 12 from Jupiter and is weak with 3 or less Bindus one becomes victim of machination, debts, diseases and enemies.

3. Ascertain the sign in which Moon has maximum Bindus. The people who have their Lagna or *Chandra* Lagna in these signs will be more helpful to the native. Hence it is better to avoid people who are born under their weak signs.

4. A strong Moon with large number of Bindus is a great asset to author, poets, writers, artists and musicians. In the horoscope of Lata Mangeshkar her Moon is in its own 3rd house of artistic abilities with 5 benefic Bindus. In the horoscope of Nargis Dutt (famous actress) Moon was in the 10th house with 7 Bindus.

Nargis Dutt
1.6.1929
5:07 AM

5. A strong Moon with good number of Bindus bestows great popularity and humanitarian personality. Mahatma Gandhi had his Moon in the 10th house with 8 Bindus. Nehru had his Moon in the Lagna with 5 Bindus in its own house.

6. One born with Moon in Kendra or Trikona and associated with 6 to 8 Bindus becomes highly learned, wealthy and powerful.

7. Good Moon is necessary for generation of wealth. Aspects of Jupiter and Mars are good for wealth.

8. A debilitated Moon with 0 to 3 Bindus destroys the house it is in. In Lagna it gives weak personality, in 4th it is neither good for property nor for Mother.

JLNehru
14.11.1889

9. Separation from Mother:

Moon is Karka for mother. Similarly 4th from Moon is taken as the house of mother. Mars in the 4th or 8th from weak Moon with less Bindus is not good for longevity of mother. Also the 8th aspect of Mars on weak Moon destroys mother.

Similarly Moon with less Bindus and Rahu in the 2nd house of *Kutumbasthan* gives ill health to mother.

10. Timing Death of Mother:

1. Multiply the Shodhya Pinda of Moon with number of Bindus in the 4th from Moon (before reduction) in the Ashtakvarga of Moon. Divide the product by 27. This gives you a Nakshatra the transit of Saturn over which or over whose trines by Saturn is not good for mother.

     Mother of Indira Gandhi Kamla Nehru fell sick in 1934 and died in February 1936. Saturn was in Nakshatra no 25 or Poorvabhadra.

SSP of Moon	= 130
Bindus in 4 from Moon	= 5
130 x 5	= 650
650 -:- 27 remainder	= 2

2. Multiply the number of Bindus in the 7th from Jupiter in the Ashtakvarga of Moon before reduction with Shodhya Pinda of Moon. Divide the product by 27. This gives you a Nakshatra the transit of Jupiter over which or over whose trines by Saturn is not good for mother. Counting of remainder is sometimes done from the Nakshatra where Jupiter is located.

3. Sometimes the figures are taken from 7th of Sun as above and transit of Sun.

4. Transit over Rashis: instead of dividing by 27, divide the above figures by 12, giving a Rashi the transit of Jupiter or Sun over which may prove fatal to mother.

11. Number of maternal uncles and aunts:

These are judged from number of Bindus in the 4th from Moon in the Ashtakvarga of Moon Male planets represent uncles, whereas female planets denote aunts.

Mental Tension: transit of Moon over the Nakshatra where 8th lord from Moon is located is not good for mental happiness.

12. All auspicious work is to be avoided on the day when Moon in Moon's Bhinnashtakvarga has contributed 0 Bindus to a Rashi. Wherever the contribution is 0 in Moon's Bhinnashtakvarga, that solar month (i.e. when Sun transits through that Rashi is not auspicious for any new work to be started and should be avoided. Suppose in Aries in the Bhinnashtakvarga of Moon there is 0 Bindu, then during the month of Aries i.e. from 13 April to 13 May, when Sun transits over Aries all auspicious works are to be avoided. Also when Moon transits over trines of Aries, Leo and Sagittarius one should avoid good work such as taking possession of a house, negotiating marriage proposals, buying a new flat or buying clothes, cutting nails and hair, etc.

13. If Moon is located in the horoscope with 1, 2 or 3 Bindus in its own Bhinnashtakvarga then one may have health problems, mental anxieties and depression, etc. This is also not good for a long life.

14. If Moon is placed in Kendra or Trikona, in its sign of debilitation Scorpio or is in inimical signs Gemini or Virgo and it is also in *Krishna Paksha* with only 2 or 3 benefic Bindus in its Bhinnashtakvarga, the strength of that Bhava is lost. If this debilitation occurs in the 5th house (in Cancer Lagna) may cause *Balarishta* or death at a young age as debilitation of

Lagna lord in the fifth with less Bindus mean loss of *Poorvapunya*. In case Moon is exalted in Kendra or Trikonas or is in friendly or own sign and is a *Shukla Paksha* Moon contributing 4 or more benefic Bindus the strength of the Bhava is increased manifold and will give excellent results.

15. If Moon has 8 benefic Bindus in its own Bhinnashtakvarga the native will be famous or may become equal to a king. With 8 benefic Bindus if in its exaltation sign and born in a King's family, he will become a *Chakravarti* i.e. the king of kings. His fame and prosperity will increase ten times. So whatever the native is, he will benefit 10 folds when the benefic Bindus are 8. If Moon's own position is good and Moon's sign is also strong the native will rise 10 to 20 times more than his present status.

16. In Moon's Bhinnashtakvarga, see which one of the trinal Rashis 1, 5, 9; 2, 6, 10; 3, 7, 11 or 4, 8, 12 is strongest or has the highest number of Bindus. Bathroom should be located in the direction, which has highest number of Bindus. These are *Kaala Purusha* Bhavas in which 1, 5, 9 signifies east; 2, 6, 10 signifies South; 3, 7, 11 signifies West; and 4, 8, 12 signifies North.

17. Also Moon's *Shodhya* Bindu is to be multiplied with Bindu of 8th Bhava from Moon and divided by 27. Remainder taken from Ashwini or its trine when transited by Moon will give anger, fights, depression moods, sorrow, etc.

18. In Moon's Bhinnashtakvarga the number of benefic Bindus in the 4th Bhava will indicate the number of co-borns for one's mother. But some astrologers say this is to be seen from Lagna only. Benefic Bindus represent number of younger co-borns of mother. Contribution by male planets means male co-borns and female planet's contribution means female co-borns. For *Shukla Paksha* Moon see from Moon and for *Krishna Paksha* Moon see from Lagna.

19. To know the longevity of one's mother, one has to see the benefic Bindus contributed in Bhinnashtakvarga of Moon. If they are more than 4 in the Bhava where Moon is placed or in the Bhava where Lagna is situated and it has benefic influence, then long life to mother may be predicted.

Profession from Moon: To know whether one is marine engineer or is having import - export business or is connected with shipping or navy, etc. add Bhinnashtakvarga Bindus of watery signs 4, 8, 12 in the Bhinnashtakvarga of Moon. Multiply the figure by Bhinnashtakvarga of Moon' Bindus. If 10th from Moon has got equal or more than these Bindus, the product is to be divided by 12 then one may have business dealing with pearl or watery products, milk products, etc. But if the total is equal to or more than 10th from Lagna then one will do business in clothes, fabrics or associated items or in wood or furniture, etc.

If the total of these watery signs divided by 12 is equal to or more than 10th Bhava from Sun, profession may be milk or milk products. One may become a teacher if it is equal to or more than 10th Bhava from Jupiter. (Note - This may not give correct results always).

Chapter 10

Ashtakvarga of Mars

1. Mars with 0 to 3 Bindus is considered weak and leads to quarrels, pessimism, and loss of status, land, property and wealth.

    Mars with 4 Bindus gives average results, whereas with 5 to 8 Bindus it gives high status, land, property, general prosperity, ability for leadership and holding a commanding position in society, having initiative, dashing personality, courage and brave mind.

    These results are augmented if Mars is exalted or its own sign and placed in Kendra or Trikona with 7 or 8 Bindus is capable of bestowing great riches, prosperity and high rank in life.

2. If Mars is exalted or is in his own house at birth and has 8 Bindus in 1, 4, 9 and 10, the native becomes a millionaire If Mars is with 4 Bindus in Aries, Leo, Scorpio, Sagittarius or Capricorn as Lagna, the native becomes a ruler.

    Please note Mars in its own house or in exaltation sign in Kendra from Lagna or Moon gives rise to Mahapurush Yoga known as Ruchaka Yoga that gives health, wealth, property, prosperity and high rank

3. Mars gives excellent results with even 4 Bindus in ascendant, 9, 5, 4 or 10 houses

    If it has more than 7 or 8 Bindus it gives high status in life.

    With 8 Bindus in Aries, Scorpio, or Capricorn as Lagna or 10th house, the native becomes a king.

4. With Mars in Lagna with 8 Bindus one becomes a big landlord.

5. Jatakadesh Marga says when Mars transits a sign in which he has 8 or maximum Bindus native gains land, wealth, gold and he performs auspicious functions. The direction indicated by that sign gives him progress in land and victory over foes.

6. In the Ashtakvarga of Mars

   i)   Count the Bindus from Lagna to Mars

   ii) Again count the Bindus from Mars to Lagna

   iii) Add the two

   In each of these three cases you get a figure, which gives you, number of year in which native suffers troubles from accidents, weapons and fire.

   Please note the period will be bad if Vimshottari Dasha also shows it. As the total Bindus of Mars are 39, it does not necessarily mean all people have trouble in 39th year.

7. The best time to buy land, property is when Mars is transiting in sign having maximum number of Bindus.

8. Transit: The transit of Mars in a Binduless Kakshaya is not good for health and personal safety. Conversely its transit in a Kakshaya where it has contributed a Bindu is good for acquiring property and generation of wealth.

9. Mars in 1, 4, 9 and 10 with 8 Bindus gives prosperity. According to Maharishi Parashara Mars in the ascendant in its own sign conjunct with or aspected by Mercury, Venus and Sun makes one very rich.

10. Mars in the 4th house is not considered bad but gives disputes in immovable property, unlawful dealings in property, etc. Agricultural income may not be there. However, Mars with 8 Bindus in the fourth house makes one very rich.

11. If Mars is placed in Lagna, 4th, 8th or 10th houses and has benefic Bindus he will be a very rich man; or if Mars is exalted with 8 benefic Bindus, he will be a *Bhoomipati*. If from Lagna Mars is in Kona i.e. 1, 5, 9 or 8, 10 and with 4 or more benefic Bindus, he will become a king or equal to a king and his earnings will be very good. We are also taking 8th and 10th because from 4th house 8th is a Trikona and 8th house Mars will aspect 2nd house and 3rd house. 3rd house deals with success through one's efforts for which connection of Mars to the 3rd house is necessary.

12. Add Bindus of 1, 5, 9; 2, 6, 10; 3, 7, 11; and 4, 8, 12; whichever group of Rashis has got the maximum number, the kitchen of the native if placed in that direction would give him good food, which will keep the native disease free, thus assuring longevity.

13. In the Bhinnashtakvarga of Mars, if in any sign the benefic Bindu contribution is 0 and if that sign, is being transited by Saturn in transit, it will cause death, death like situations, diseases, enmity, property disputes, court cases, etc. to one's co-born. This has to be seen in relation to Dasha/Antardasha of the native is concerned. If the Dasha is good and only the transit is bad, then it is only loss of wealth. If both are bad, may cause death of co-born. Some astrologers are of the view that 3rd house is seen for younger co-borns and 11th for elder co-borns.

14. Retention capacity depends on Mars because he is *Bhoomi Putra* and signifies permanency in any thing i.e. wealth, fame, etc. Mars' contribution is a must. If it has not contributed any benefic Bindus in Lagna, 5th house, 9th house etc. it is very bad.

15. For knowing the status or position of co-borns take the Bindu of 3rd from Mars and the Bindu of 3rd from Lagna, multiply. If the product is equal to or more than the sum total of Lagna Bhava and 10H; 9H and 5H; 6H and 2H; 11H and 8H; then

the native's co-born is considered to be well placed than self, father, uncle (maternal & paternal) and elder brother respectively.

16. A person may be having business dealings in surgical instruments or hospital items if the total of Bindu in Bhavas where Moon, Mars and 10H equals to the total of Lagna Bhava, 6H and 11H. Secondly, a person will become a thief or an anti-social element if the Bindu contribution of Mars, Saturn and Sun are equal to or more than 8th, 12th and 3rd Bhava.

17. If Mars in the natal chart is conjoined with Rahu or placed in the Nakshatra of Rahu or Saturn is placed in the Nakshatra of Rahu or Mars with good number of Bindus; a person will become an administrator (IAS), Police or Army Officer.

18. A person will have good landed property or he may get ancestral property if the Bindu of 4th from Mars and 4th from Lagna are added and its Bindus are more than Lagna Bhava and 8th Bhava total or Lagna Bhava and 8th Bhava total from Mars.

19. For inheritance from father, see the 8th house from Mars. Multiply the total of Bindus from Mars to the 8th house with Bindus of the 8th lord and divide by 27. Counting from Ashwini/Dhanishta whenever Jupiter transits through the remainder Nakshatra inheritance will occur. Involvement of Mars or the 8th lord is necessary for inheritance.

20. **Mangal or Kuja Dosha:**

    Mangal or Kuja Dosha is seen from Lagna, Moon or Venus. If Mars is located in Lagna, 2nd house, 4th, 7th, 8th or 12th, then it is considered to be *Mangala Dosha*. In South India 2nd is more important which is also taken as *Mangala Dosha*. In earlier times, this was followed everywhere. In earlier times Mangala Dosha was considered to be most malefic from Venus, then from Lagna and least from Moon. But, now-a-days, it is seen from Lagna only. Mars is the Karaka for the

8th Bhava. Owning the 8th house of Kaala Purusha, it becomes the Karaka for sexual pleasures and thus for sexual parts also. If Mars is in the 8th Bhava from Lagna or Venus, one will have more involvement in sexual pleasures of life. Thus equal matching should be done so that tension does not prevail between the couple, since this could be the main cause of marital problems. Also since Mars is in the 8th house, any kind of secret desires or perversions of a person could be seen from the position of Mars. If this *Dosha* is not matched or is not found equal in both the horoscopes, one's atrocious or dominance over the other will be manifold. For this purpose, it is only this *Dosha* that should be present in both the horoscopes. The most malefic Bhava are the 7th and 8th. If a native has Mars in 7th or 8th house from Lagna or Moon it should be matched equally with the same kind of horoscope where Mars is in 7th or 8th from Lagna or Moon. If it is Lagna Bhava, some people say it is not a *Dosha* at all or it is very less here. The 8th house contributes to longevity of a native and for females it is the longevity of her husband. If Mars is placed in this Bhava it also affects the longevity of the other partner or will inflict disease upon the other partner. If the longevity of one partner is good and if one has Mangala Dosha and the other not, the other partner will always be sick.

For the purpose of seeing *Mangala Dosha* the contribution of *Rekha* (Malefic Rekhas) in Lagna, 2nd house, 4th house, 7th house, 8th and 12th houses are to be seen. If the contribution of Rekha by Lagna, Moon and Venus from Mars in these Bhavas are more than benefic Bindus then Mangala Dosha prevails. If Mars is placed in Lagna, 2nd, 4th, 7th, 8th or 12th houses ascertain if the malefic Rekhas contributed by Lagna, Moon, Venus are more than benefic Bindus present there. If so then Mangala Dosha is considered to the maximum. This position is to be seen from Prastharashtaka Varga. Here also 7th and 8th Bhava is to be seen giving greater importance to these Bhavas. If the contributions of malefic Rekhas are more from all the three planets, one will have separation, widowhood/

widower hood, loss of seminal fluids and sexual diseases. If in the 2nd house from Mars the malefic *Rekhas* contributed by Lagna, Moon, Venus and 2nd lord are more than the benefic Bindus one will have more than one wife and there will be problems in marital life. Wife will also dominate her husband.

If the contribution of malefic Rekhas are more in the 4th Bhava in the Bhinnashtakvarga of Mars by all five, Lagna, Moon, Venus, 4th lord and Mars one will have enmity towards his mother or loss of paternal property. In the 12th house we take the contribution of malefic Rekhas by Lagna, Moon, Venus, 12th lord which causes lack of sexual pleasures.

Mars – Saturn: Mars with 5 Bindus conjunct or aspected by Saturn gives a Rajyoga. (Normally, Mars Saturn combination is not considered good).

Mars – Mercury Combination:

Weak Mars with less Bindus is neither good for finances nor for healthy sexual life.

With Mercury, weak Mars gives break in education Similarly Mars in 2nd from Mercury causes dislocation in studies.

Number of Brothers and Sisters:

This is known from the number of Bindus in the third from Mars in the Ashtakvarga of Mars before reduction. Bindus contributed by male planets represent brothers while Bindus by female planets denotes sisters. In this omit the figures contributed by inimical and debilitated planets.

Denial of Brothers:

It is stated in the classical books that position of Mars with more than 6 Bindus in 3, 6, 8, 11, and 12 houses is not good for brothers unless there are benefic aspects.

Sickness or death of Brothers:

Sickness, death or bad time for brothers:

1. Multiply the Shodhya Pinda of Mars with number of Bindus in the 3rd from Mars (before reduction) in the Ashtakvarga of Mars. Divide the product by 27. This gives you a Nakshatra the transit of Saturn over which or over whose trines is not good for brothers.

2. Multiply the number of Bindus in the 7th from Jupiter in the Ashtakvarga of Mars before reduction with Shodhya Pinda of Mars. Divide the product by 27. This gives you a Nakshatra the transit of Jupiter over which or over whose trines is not good for brother. Counting of remainder is sometimes done from the Nakshatra where Jupiter is located.

3. Sometimes the figures are taken from 7th of Sun as above and transit of Sun watched.

4. Transit over Rashis: if instead of dividing by 27, you divide the above figures by 12, this gives you a Rashi the transit of Jupiter or Sun over which may prove fatal for brother.

Period of Prosperity for Brothers:

Multiply the Shodhya Pinda of Mars with the figures in the 3rd from Mars and divide the product by 12. The resultant figure will denote a Rashi counted from Aries, the transit of Jupiter over which will prove beneficial to brothers.

No indication is given as to which brother is going to prosper. We have to make use of relevant horoscopes of brothers.

Sickness or Death of Brothers without use of Shodhya Pinda:

Total the number of Bindus in the Ashtakvarga of Mars after two reductions. Multiply this by figures in the 3rd from Mars and divide the product by 27. The remainder gives you a figure which when counted from Ashwini gives you a Nakshatra the transit over which or over whose trines by Saturn is not good for brothers.

Chapter 11

Ashtakvarga of Mercury

With 0 to 3 Bindus Mercury will be weak and it gives loss of wealth, lack of intelligence and unhappy relation with family members and friends. Mercury having 0 to 3 Bindus and placed in 6 or 8 house without any benefic aspects, the person become unreliable and crooked in his behavior. Whereas Mercury with 5 to 8 Bindus and placed in Kendra or Trikona with aspects of Jupiter or Saturn, the person becomes highly learned and powerful speaker. With 4 Bindus it considered to be of average.

Mercury

1. Mercury with 4 Bindus in signs of Mars and Navamsa of Venus, aspected by Jupiter makes a person writer, poet, dramatist or literary figure.

2. Mercury in Kendra or Trikona with 5 or more Bindus with aspect, of Jupiter or Saturn makes one learned in scriptures.

3. Mercury with 5 Bindus with Jupiter or Mars makes one a scientist.

4. Four or more Bindus in 2nd from Mercury in to Ashtakvarga of Mercury makes one a great speaker.

5. Seven or more Bindus in 2nd from Mercury makes one poet and a great orator.

6. It is possible to judge the type of speaker one is from Bindus contributed by planets in 2nd from Mercury. The malefic makes

them boastful and full of false promises. Jupiter makes one noble and gives spiritual talk, Venus artistic, Mercury humorous and Moon romantic and delightful talk. Saturn gives falsehood and Sun boastful talk. Mars makes one rude, angry, abusive and braggadocio.

7. Literary achievements should be seen in 5th from Mercury. Swami Vivekananda had 7 Bindus in 5th from Mercury in Ashtakvarga of Mercury.

8. Mercury with 4 and more Bindus with malefic and debilitated in Navamsa gives proficiency in dance, drama and music.

Dispositor of Mercury: If lord of the sign in which Mercury is placed is in Kendra or Trikona with many Bindus, one gets name, fame and prosperity. If lord is in 6, 8 or 12 there is break in education.

Combinations for an Astrologer:

1. Aspect of Jupiter on the 2nd.

2. Mercury with 5 Bindus in 4, 6, or 10 from Saturn.

3. Ketu with 3 Bindus in the Ashtakvarga of Mercury in the 5th house or with lord of 5th.

Setback in Business: Multiply the Shodhya Pinda of Mercury with figures in the 10th from Mercury in the Ashtakvarga of Mercury before reduction. Divide the product by 27 and get the remainder. This remainder gives a Nakshatra, the transit of Saturn over which or over whose trines gives a setback or problems in business.

Period of Mental Agony: Multiply the Shodhya Pinda of Mercury with figures in the 4th from Mercury in the Ashtakvarga of Mercury before reduction. Divide the product by 27 and get the remainder. This remainder gives you a Nakshatra over which or whose trines, the transit of Saturn gives period of mental agony.

Good Period for Education and friendship:

Multiply the Shodhya Pinda of Mercury with figures in the 4th from Mercury in the Ashtakvarga of Mercury before reduction. Divide the product by 12. The remainder gives a Rashi the transit of Jupiter over which or whose trines gives good results.

Placed in Kendras or Trikonas with 8 Bindus one is well versed in family traditions, is very lucky and rises very high in family's traditional business.

Mercury is the Karaka for education. As such the solar month in which it gives maximum benefic Bindus will prove best for starting education.

Loss of wealth is caused when Saturn transits over a Rashi where Mercury has made no contribution.

Add total Bindus in (1, 5, 9; 2, 6, 10; 3, 7, 11 and 4, 8, 12) houses. Whichever Rashi has maximum Bindus, in that direction the native's playground or study room should be located.

If the trine houses from Mercury have more than 5 benefic Bindus one will be well read. Person will have great understanding ability, and if it has aspect of Jupiter also one may rises high in educational field.

A person will become a sculptor or a mathematician if the 2nd Bhava from Mercury has got more than 5 benefic Bindus and the 2L is not afflicted.

If the dispositor of Mercury is in trine and Mercury has 5 or more benefic Bindus then again a person will be very intelligent, learned and able administrator.

For marriage purposes, affliction to Mercury is not good. Weak Mercury's connection with 7th Bhava or 7th lord or depositor of 7L indicates a person whose spouse will run away or who may desert her husband or his wife may have an indifferent attitude towards the native.

The position of Mercury in a female chart is to be very minutely considered. If Mercury has no Bindu and is afflicted, kindness and sense of mercy will be missing. She may even murder her own husband or children for the sake of a paramour. The 7th Bhava from Lagna in the Bhinnashtakvarga of Mercury and 7H from Venus should have more benefic Bindus otherwise kindness from spouse is missing.

Add Bindu of the 2nd, 5th and 10th Bhavas from Mercury and compare these with total of Lagna, 9th Bhava and 11th Bhavas. If they are equal then a person will have earnings from or inclination towards writing, invoking or talking to spirits

Chapter 12

Ashtakvarga of Jupiter

Transit of Jupiter in signs with less than 3 Bindus in its own Ashtakvarga is not auspicious. It gives loss of wealth, health, trouble for relatives and problem with government.

With 4 Bindus results are average.

5 to 6 Bindus gives success and gain of wealth.

With 7 to 8 Bindus one gets fame, happiness and riches.

Jupiter, well placed in the horoscope with more than 5 Bindus is an asset. Even if Jupiter is in houses 6, 8 or 12, and has five or more Bindus, one has wealth and long life and gains victory over his enemies.

In the Bhinnashtakvarga of Jupiter in whichever Rashi he has contributed maximum number of Bindus or in whichever group of Rashis it has the maximum Bindus, in that direction one should keep jewelry, treasures, food grains, etc.

If Sun has got less benefic Bindus in the Bhinnashtakvarga of Jupiter, any venture undertaken by a native for his progress will meet with obstacles.

Jupiter in 6th, 8th or 12th Bhava with 5 or more benefic Bindus will give *poornayu* to the native; will give wealth and happiness and capacity to win over his enemies. Jupiter in 6th, 7th or 8th from Moon or Lagna forms Adhi Yoga. One will have the capacity to win over others if Jupiter is in the 6th; will be able and give public appearance if in the 7th; and will give long life if in the 8th. The same results will follow if all the three benefics i.e. Jupiter, Mercury and Venus are in 6th, 7th and 8th from Moon.

Fifth from Jupiter should also be strong as *Bhavat Bhava* should always be powerful. So from where Jupiter is placed, if 5th has 5 or more benefic Bindus, a person will have prosperity, long life, attractive personality. He will be a leader.

If Jupiter has got 8 benefic Bindus and is not afflicted and is posited with Moon or in Kendra to Moon, the person will be good looking, will be wealthy, will have able progeny. With 6 benefic Bindus and posited together with Moon or in Kendra to Moon, he will have a number of vehicles and will be very rich.

i.   If Jupiter is in 6, 8 and 12 with more than 6 Bindus, it makes a person king or equal to king.

ii. If Jupiter is in Kendra / Trikona with 7 or 8 Bindus and is not with any debilitated or combust planet in Rashis other than that Mercury or Venus it gives many wives and children.

iii. Planet in Dasha, Antar, or Gochar if has more than 5 Bindus gives effect of Yogkarka. Jupiter as 6 lord in 8 gives much wealth.

Timing Birth of Children:

Multiply the Shodhya Pinda of Jupiter by the number of Bindus in the 5th from Jupiter in the Ashtakvarga of Jupiter before reduction. Divide the product by 27. It gives you a remainder which represents the Nakshatra transit of Saturn over whom or over whose trines is bad for the health of children.

Timing Birth of Children II

Conception takes place during transit of Jupiter over;

i)   A sign carrying high number of Bindus

ii) Rashi or Navamsa of 5th lord from Lagna, Moon or Jupiter.

iii) Rashi or Navamsa of Gulika.

iv) Conception also takes place when Sun is transiting in a sign having maximum number of Bindus in Jupiter's Ashtakvarga.

v)   Mating when the sign having maximum number of Bindus in Jupiter's Ashtakvarga is rising, is good for conception and birth of a son.

Virtuous Son

If dispositor of 5th lord is associated with Jupiter having 4 or more Bindus a worthy son is born.

Yogas for ungrateful children and grand children

1.   5th lord having connection with 8th lord without any aspect of Jupiter.

2.   5th house / lord afflicted by malefic, Jupiter with less than three Bindus and Jupiter in Papkartari Yoga

Fifth Bhava is for progeny and is controlled by Jupiter. In the Bhinnashtakvarga of Jupiter the Bhava where Jupiter is placed or the Bhava which gets the maximum number of benefic Bindus, that Bhava indicates the sex of the child. Suppose in the Bhinnashtakvarga of Jupiter, Mithuna has the maximum number of benefic Bindus say 7. Due to 7 benefic Bindus whenever Mithuna is transited by male planets like Sun, Mars or Jupiter itself, will indicate time co-relating to time conception or delivery of a child, it is related with 9th Bhava, as 9th Bhava indicates Bhagya. When transited by male planets it indicates male progeny and when transited by female planets will indicate female progeny. Saturn and Mercury are eunuchs. Saturn transits over a Rashi for two-and-a-half years and may not get connected to the 9th Bhava from there. So Saturn has to be taken on the basis of Nakshatra it is placed in. For every Nakshatra that Saturn transits over he gives a different result.

Profession: Jupiter represents business in gold and silver jwellery, gems, government service or in public sector undertakings as it is *Rajgraha*. It also represents law and judiciary printing and publishing of books on religion. In the Bhinnashtakvarga of Jupiter, Bindus where Jupiter is placed is to be multiplied with Bindus in the 2H and 10H Bindus are to be added. If the total is equal to 11th Bhava's Sarvashtakvarga then one will earn profit out of his business. If equal to or more than 10H Bindus one will be doing only business.

Spirituality and Jupiter's Bhinnashtakvarga

Connection of Mercury and Ketu with Jupiter is good for spiritualism and attaining Siddhi means getting control over our inner self and achieving oneness with Atma, Jeevatma and Parmatma. Jupiter plays a very important role in attainment of Siddhi. In the Bhinnashtakvarga of Jupiter, if 5 or more benefic Bindus are in the 5th from Lagna, or in the 5th from where Jupiter is placed or in the house where Ketu is placed (though Ketu does not qualify as a planet for Ashtakvarga. For prediction purposes placement of Ketu can be considered) one will have mantra Siddhi. Such a Siddhi will be of Saumya Devtas if it is being aspected or conjoined with Sun or in the Rashi of Sun or in the Rashi of Jupiter himself or in the Rashi of Venus.

For Mantra Siddhi 5H, 5L, 5th from Jupiter and Jupiter himself all should have 5 or more benefic Bindus. If in the 5H from Lagna or even 5th from Jupiter in the Sarvashtakvarga has more than 25 benefic Bindus, one will have inclination towards mantra Siddhi. In Sarvashtakvarga if these Rashis have more than 30 Bindus, one will perform mantra Siddhi with the help of Yantras. If more than 35 Bindus, one will have extra-ordinary powers to cure others through mantra Siddhi.

If it is in the Rashi of Saturn or in the negative Rashi of Mars one will have Mantra Siddhi of low Devtas or Shudra Devtas. If Rahu or afflicted Saturn is present, then one will use his mantra Siddhi in a malefic way or for foul means like voodoo, tantra, etc.

Guru: To become a preceptor or to have a preceptor, 9th house from Jupiter, 9th house from Lagna and Sun himself, if all possess atleast 5 or more than 5 Bindus in the Bhinnashtakvarga of Jupiter. If these houses are connected to the Lagna or Mercury, then one will become a guru himself. Connection of Lagna Lord and Jupiter; Lagna Lord and Mercury or Lagna Lord in the 9th house; or if these Bhavas are connected to Venus or Lagna Lord, one will have a guru.

Deity for an Individual: Deity for worship has to be seen from the 5th house keeping in view that the Adhi Devta for Sun is Lord Shiva or Sun God; for Moon - Gauri; Mars - Kartikeya or Hanuman; Mercury - Vishnu or his Avtaras; Jupiter - Lord Shiva, Vishnu and Brahma or Dattatreya; Venus - Mahalaxmi or Saraswati; Saturn - Lord Shiva or Bhairav; Rahu - Mahashakti or Serpent; and Ketu - Ganapati. The planet which influences the 5th house to the maximum and is very powerful in his own Bhinnashtakvarga contributing 5 or more Bindus will indicate the deity one should be worshipping.

The following position may be seen:

1.   Planet most powerfully influencing the 5H;

2.   If that planet has inherent strength as owner of a Bhava;

3.   Contribution to the 5th Bhava from Lagna in the Bhinnashtakvarga of that particular planet should be 5 or more;

4.   If there is no planet aspecting 5H or influencing the 5H then we have to take the 5L where he is placed.

5.   If the 5L is also not aspecting the 5H and getting no connection whatsoever, then we have to see the 5L himself. In the Bhinnashtakvarga of 5L contribution in the 5th from Lagna has to be seen. Secondly, wherever he is placed; and thirdly 5H from the 5L. All these should not have great parity and should have more than 5 Bindus in any case.

6.   Lastly, we take the dispositor of the 5L and find out who is stronger between the 5L and its dispositor.

Benefit From Studies:

If Kendra from Lagna or Konas from Jupiter or Upachaya Sthana and has got more than 4 Bindus, then a native's permanency in studies/Vinaya will be indicated. Kendras are the pillars of a horoscope and should be strong. Likewise, if the Konas in D-1 becomes Kendras from Jupiter getting 5 or more Bindus then also a native will benefit from studies. Position of Mercury has to be seen. Mercury should contribute not less than 4 in Kendras from Jupiter in the Bhinnashtakvarga of Mercury.

Chapter 13

Ashtakvarga of Venus

Venus associated with 0 to 3 Bindus, combust, debilitated, placed in 6, 8 and 12 and aspected by malefic, causes all kinds of troubles It causes diseases, loss of property, quarrels with wife, unpopularity with woman, enmity with female bosses, quarrel with neighbors

With 4 Bindus it gives mixed results, neither good nor bad.

With 5 to 8 Bindus it gives wealth, prosperity, women, conveyances, houses, bed pleasures, art, music, mirth and happiness.

1. Venus with 4 or more Bindus, exalted Navamsa, aspect of Mars, vitality till old age.

    Venus in 6, 8, or 12 less than 3 Bindus causes rape and unnatural sexual offences.

2. Venus with 5 to 8 Bindus in Kendras or Trikonas, makes one a commander in the army. He has conveyances and is rich.

3. According to Jatakadesh Marga, Venus transiting in a sign having highest number of Bindus gives furnishing for bed chamber, knowledge for music, performance of marriages, sensual enjoyment and much prosperity.

4. An unafflicted Venus with many Bindus is a great asset for happy married life.

5. If lord of the sign occupied by Venus is associated with 5 or more Bindus it gives all kinds of wealth, happiness and comforts.

6. Venus in signs of Mars with 5 or more Bindus gives much wealth.

7. Transit of Venus through a Kakshaya having Bindus in her Ashtakvarga given one elevation in status, birth of a daughter, wealth, popularity with other sex, sports, etc.

    While transiting through a Kakshaya with no Bindu, loss of wealth and trouble to wife will occur.

8. With more than five Bindus in Lagna, Venus gives a charming personality.

9. In Kendra, well placed and more Bindus person is attractive, artistic and fond of music.

Timing of Marriage:

Indira Gandhi was married on 25 March 1942.

Multiply the Shodhya Pinda of Venus with the number of Bindus in the 7th from Venus. Divide the product by 27. When Jupiter transits the Nakshatra represented by remainder or its trine, marriage is likely.

Month of Marriage:

Multiply the Shodhya Pinda of Venus with the number of Bindus in the 7th from Sun in the Ashtakvarga of Venus. Divide the product by 12. When Sun transits the sign represented by remainder or its trine, marriage is likely, if Dasha / Antardashas is also favourable.

Death or Agony to Partner:

Multiply the Shodhya Pinda of Venus with the number of Bindus in the 7th from Venus. Divide the product by 27. When Saturn transits the Nakshatra represented by remainder or its trine hardship to wife occurs. She may even die if Dasha so warrants.

Other Predictions of Venus through Ashtakvarga

With 8 Bindus in Kendra or Trikona a person becomes a, warrior, or a commander in the armed forces. In the Airy signs it takes one to the Air Force, while in fiery signs one may be chief in the army. A watery sign he will become chief of Navy.

With Venus strong one may have many vehicles at his command as Venus is Karka for vehicles. In Ketu's Nakshatra or with Ketu two wheelers are indicated.

If Venus is in a Kendra or Kona with 7 benefic Bindus it indicates Dheergayu. Ayu is taken here because for Kaala Purusha Venus is the 2nd & 7th lord and also being the *Asura* Guru, so both the *Maraka* qualities are with Venus. Thus Venus becomes three-fourth benefic and not a full benefic. He is a natural Marakesh. With 7 benefic Bindus one is ostentatious. If Venus is in debilitation or in the 7th, 8th or 12th Bhava and also possessing 7 or 8 benefic Bindus, this is not considered as a good position.

Bedroom should be located in the direction in which a Bhava has maximum Bindus in the Bhinnashtakvarga of Venus. Maximum Bindus are necessary for controlling women and having better sexual life. If maximum Bindus are in two or three Bhavas then choose the Bhava after reductions. Whichever Bhava gains strength, and in whichever Bhavas there are maximum Bindus, one should have his bed-room in that direction to have a better sleep and sexual life. This is the reason why Venus should have more benefic Bindus and also 7H should have lesser Bindus than Lagna Bhava otherwise the females will control him. If such a Venus has the influence of Mars, then one will be amorous.

Add the Bindus in 1, 5, 9/ 2, 6, 10 /3, 7, 11 /4, 8, 12. Whichever trinal group has maximum Bindus, in that direction there should be bedroom. According to *Vaastu Shastra,* the bedroom should be located in South-west direction. In case it is not possible to do so, one may have the bed in south west direction of the house/room.

The transit of Venus in the sign having maximum Bindus in its Bhinnashtakvarga will give association with females, purchase of land, property, wealth and enjoyments.

Profession from Venus Bhinnashtakvarga: Venus indicates audio-visuals, art, artistic, handicrafts, export of clothes, textiles, artificial flowers, Ikebana, painting, computer-graphics (Venus with Rahu-Ketu - here Rahu, Ketu is for computers and Venus for graphics). Mars should also be strong, because computers run on electricity. These indications are true when 10th from Venus gets good number of benefic Bindus in Venus Bhinnashtakvarga. The 10th Bhava from Lagna in the Sarvashtakvarga should match with the sum total of Bindus in 10H, 11H and 2H in Venus Bhinnashtakvarga. Some astrologers believe that after taking the sum total of 10th, 11th and 2nd in Venus Bhinnashtakvarga, multiply it with the Bindus of wherever Venus is placed and deduct the total number of Bindus of 10th lord's Bhinnashtakvarga from the product. If this related to profession.

If the 3rd, 7th and 11th Bhavas have got any similarity to the 10th house in the Sarvashtakvarga total and if they are perfectly divisible then one will have also Venus related profession.

To analyse the 4th Bhava, multiply the Shodhya Pinda of Venus with the Bindus in 4th from Venus. If this is similar to the Sarvashtakvarga of 4th Bhava then one will have a good house. Thus we can judge any Bhava by multiplying the Shodhya Pinda of that Bhava from Venus in Venus Bhinnashtakvarga and comparing it with Sarvashtakvarga Bindus in that particular Bhava.

Count the number of benefic Bindus in the Bhinnashtakvarga of Venus from Lagna to the Bhava where Venus is placed. The resultant number will indicate the age at which one will get a house, enjoyment etc.

Add the Bindus in the 4th, 5th and 9th houses from Venus in the Bhinnashtakvarga of Venus, if this relates to the 4th Bhava in Sarvashtakvarga then earnings out of one's property is indicated. If the 8th house is stronger, one may have trouble from his rented property.

In Bhinnashtakvarga if a planet has 4 Bindus, loss and gain will occur simultaneously including happiness and possessions of wealth. If Venus is contributing 4 Bindus in the 4th house from Lagna, during the dasha of Venus and the Antardasha of 4th from Venus he will give *Vahana Sukha* to the native, but may cause accidents also. For any Bhava or Karaka we have to see the Bhavat-Bhava which is a shadow house and confirms a good or bad happening. We also have to work out exactly the quantum of malefic influence generated.

If a planet has contributed 5 benefic Bindus, one will have all types of happiness in the family, meeting with saintly persons pilgrimages, gain in higher studies, gains from speculation, marriage of the native or a close relative, etc. We will see this according to the transit of the particular Karaka on that Bhava. If the benefic Bindus are 6, then a person may have imposing personality, will be good looking, well mannered, will easily win over enemies, will be free from debts and diseases. If more than 7, it gives *Vahana Sukha, Aishwarya,* luxuries, material happiness. With eight Bindus he is a king.

If a planet contributes only 0 Bindus, the result will be bad only. He will be devoid of strength as far as Ashtakvarga is concerned. Let us take Venus. Suppose Venus is placed in the 3H from Lagna and in the 5th from the 3H he has 0 benefic Bindus i.e. Venus has not given any Bindus in the 7H (5th from 3H is the 7H). Since 5H also promises marriage and 7H being the house of spouse also, as far as counting of Bindus go, if Venus is not contributing anything firstly there is no marriage or no wife at all. Venus contributing to any Bhava is good. His contributing no Bindus at all is not good because it is the Karaka for enjoyments.

Multiply the Bindus in the Sarvashtakvarga of 7th house with the 7L's contribution in his Bhinnashtakvarga in that Bhava and divide by 27. Count the reminder from Ashwini for a benefic Moon (Shukla Paksha) and from Dhanishta for a malefic Moon (Krishna Paksha). If it comes to that Rashi where the Nakshatra of 7L is placed, the native will not marry at all. Contribution of a planet if it coincides with that particular Bhava from Lagna further aggravates problems.

Chapter 14

Ashtakvarga of Saturn

Saturn is Karka for death, disease and sorrow. It causes delays hindrances, poverty, separation, jealousy and perversion.

A strong Saturn on the other hand is good for hard work, concentration, endurance and spiritual life. It also is a Karka for agriculture land, fixed assets and property.

Result of Transit of Saturn

Transit of Saturn in a Bhava with 0 to 3 Bindus cause disease, financial loss, worries from low caste, lot of hard work but less gain, trouble to wife and children losses or death like situation for the native.

In a Bhava with 4 Bindus it gives neutral results. However, since Saturn has only maximum of 37 points in its own Bhinnashtakvarga, it has been observed that 4 Bindus give adequate strength.

In a Bhava with 5 to 8 Bindus Saturn makes one leader of masses, gives wealth and dominance over others.

Same results have been attributed by some writers to a natal Saturn with different number of Bindus. We have not found this to be reliable interpretation. Obviously much and more research will have to be done before arriving at sound conclusions.

While analyzing the result of transit, the basic rules of astrology should be kept in mind. The transit of Saturn in 3, 6, and 11 Bhava from Moon Lagna gives good results provided it has good number of Bindus. The period of Saade Saati could be period of trouble and mantel worries, if Dasha is also bad. So is the case of transit of Saturn in 4th and 8th house from Lagna and Moon. If the relevant Bhava in Sarvashtakvarga have more than 28 Bindus, the transit of Saturn may not give bad results.

It has been stated in classical books that if Saturn is strong in Lagna with 6 benefic bindus, it indicates that a native will always be sorrowful in life and other will not understand him. In exaltation it will make person philosophical, detached while losing everything in life including parental property. (This may not be true in actual practice as a strong Saturn in its own sign or sign of exaltation in Lagna give Mahapurusha Yoga with all the prosperity and wealth).

Saturn in debilitation or in inimical sign with 5 or more benefic Bindus with a strong Moon gives *Poornayu*. One has to see the strength of Moon also for predicting *poornayu*.

If trinal lord of any Rashi is Moon or Saturn the native with such Rashi will have less trouble with *Saade Saati*. For Pisces born natives Cancer is a trinal Rashi, and hence less troublesome. Likewise for Tula Rashi, Saturn is a trinal lord and will never give any trouble.

Saturn in Lagna or 5th Bhava and in inimical sign or debilitated or combust or lost in planetary war with 4 or less benefic Bindus indicates association with immoral women, servants and shows little wealth. It there are 8 benefic Bindus, the native will have leadership qualities and will control a holy place where Mantras are chanted as also Yagna, Yantra Pooja and Tantra Poojas are performed. With 7 benefic Bindus one will be wealthy and rich.

Add the total bindus in 1, 5, 9 / 2, 6, 10 / 3, 7, 11 / 4, 8, 12 in the Bhinnashtakvarga of Saturn. Which group has more bindus; in that direction one should have his dust bin or waste room.

In the Bhinnashtakvarga of Saturn where there are less or no benefic Bindus, transit of Sun and Moon over that Rashi also indicates death during that solar month. (For Makara and Kumbha

Lagna natives Sun and Moon become the 7th lords.)

Count the benefic Bindus from Saturn to Lagna and from Lagna to Saturn and add the two. The total will represent the year when one will have diseases, debts and mental trouble.

Transit of Saturn in Kakshaya

The transit of Saturn in a Bindu less Kakshaya causes loss of health and wealth, misery, sorrow and may lead to accident.

The transit of Saturn in a Kakshaya having Bindu in his Ashtakvarga gives inheritance, victory, agriculture products, land and contracts with the government.

Good time to start agriculture works

The good time to acquire servants and start agriculture works would be when Saturn is transiting over house having good number of Bindus. But since Saturn is a slow moving planet, this rule is not of much use in practical application, as Saturn would be transiting in strongest house once in 30 years, so it is better to start the work at the time when Lagna is rising with maximum number of Bindus.

Short Life

It has been stated in the text books that exalted Saturn placed in a Kendra and having 1 to 4 Bindus gives short life. It has also been stated that a strong Saturn having 5 to 6 Bindus and located in the first house causes much misery and short life and loss of wealth. However, a debilitated Saturn or when it is placed in enemy house, if associated with 5 or more Bindus give good results provided Moon is well placed.

We have not found this principle to be valid. The basic rule that Saturn placed in Kendra in its own house or in exaltation sign gives rise to Mahapurusha Yoga (Sassa Yoga) in more valid. The more the numbers of Bindus, the better are the results.

If the Saturn in Lagna or in the 4th is not placed in own house or exaltation sign and associated with less number of Bindus, it is not conducive to long life. Being Karaka for 'Ayu ' and being weak, as also having malefic aspect at Lagna, it could be partly true, but for short life, other factors like absence of benefices in Kendras, weak Lagna lord, weak Moon and Jupiter as also afflicted 8th and 10th houses/lords are important factors which must be taken into account before judgment on short life is pronounced.

It has also been stated in the texts that debilitated Saturn in Lagna or in an inimical house with more than 4 Bindus and aspected by benefices give long life.

Combinations for Prosperity

1. Mahapurusha Yoga (Sassa Yoga). When Saturn is in Kendra from Lagna or Moon in its own or exalted sign gives plenty of power and wealth.

2. Benefices in the 8th from Lagna or Saturn and lord of that house if strong, bestows immense riches and happiness.

3. In Taurus Lagna, where Saturn is a Yoga Karaka, being a lord of 9th and 10th, if placed in 3rd, 6th or 11th associated with 3 Bindus gives rise to a powerful Rajyoga.

4. A combust Saturn when debilitated or in enemy sign in Lagna or 5th house, in some cases other houses also and associated with 4 or 5 Bindus gives plenty of wealth. The more the number of Bindus higher the amount of prosperity and accompanying paraphernalia like plenty of servants, concubines etc.

5. If Saturn and Moon in Lagna having more than 4 Bindus is combination for poverty but in other Kendras it gives prosperity and Rajyoga.

Adverse Combinations

1. Saturn in 2nd or 12th in its own sign (Capricorn or Aquarius Lagna), and other malefic in Trikona give poverty, provided

Saturn is with 4 Bindus.

2.   Lord of 8th from Saturn or Lagna combust or in enemy sign and has no benefic aspects.

3.   Debilitated Saturn and Exalted Mars, each with 4 Bindus in Saturn's Ashtakvarga and lord of 8th house is weak give poverty.

Transit of Saturn and death:

Multiply the Shodhya Pinda of Saturn with figure in the 8th from Saturn (in some books say a figure in the 7th from Saturn) in the Ashtakvarga of Saturn before reduction. Divide the product by 27, the remainder gives a Nakshatra, the transit of Saturn over which or its Trines could be fatal for the native.

Example of Indira Gandhi

SP of Saturn in 196 x 1 =196 -:- 27 = 7 is remainder. Saturn was transiting in Vishakha, which is Trine Nakshatra of Punarvasu counted from Ashwini, when she was shot dead.

Or

Multiply the Shodhya Pinda of Saturn with the number of Bindus in the sign occupied by Saturn in the Ashtakvarga of Saturn before reduction. Divide the product by 27, the remainder gives a Nakshatra, the transit of Saturn over which or its Trines could be fatal for the native.

Or

Multiply the Shodhya Pinda of Saturn with the number of Bindus in the sign occupied by Jupiter in the Ashtakvarga of Saturn before reduction. Divide the product by 12, the remainder gives a Rashi, the transit of Saturn over which or its Trines could be fatal for the native.

Shodhya Pinda of Saturn and transit of Sun

Multiply the Shodhya Pinda of Saturn with the number of Bindus in the sign occupied by Sun in the Ashtakvarga of Saturn before reduction. Divide the product by 12, the remainder gives a Rashi, the transit of Sun over which or its Trines could be fatal for the native.

Chapter 15

Ashtakvarga and Transit

Planetary movements i.e. stay in one Rashi

Planets	Sun	Moon	Mars	Mercury	Jupiter	Venus	Saturn	Rahu
In Rashi	30 days	2.25 days	45 days	28 days	1 year	30 days	2.5 years	1.5 years

Per day means motion of the planets:-

As per ancient Astronomical Books							As per Modern Astronomical
Planet	0	/	//	Para	Para-tpara	Tat Para	0 - / - // - ///
Saturn	00	02	00	22	53	25	0 – 02 – 01.9
Jupiter	00	04	59	8	48	35	0 – 04 – 59.1
Mars	00	31	26	28	11	09	0 – 31 – 26.5
Sun	00	59	08	10	10	24	0 – 59 – 08.2
Venus	01	36	07	43	37	15	1 – 36 – 07.7
Mercury	04	05	32	20	41	51	04 – 05 – 32.4
Moon	13	10	34	52	03	49	13 – 10 – 35.0

It should be remembered that results of transit cannot take precedence over those promised in the birth chart. The birth horoscope is the main important chart containing the Dasha scheme binding us all the grand design of Karma. The whole scheme of destiny is nothing else but the unfolding of Karmas. The good or bad events that occur in our life are the fruits of our Karma.

For example if children are not promised in the horoscope then however results may be good in transit, birth of children must not predict. In fact transits should be given secondary importance to main events promised in Dasha scheme.

While primary importance is given to Dasha then to transit combined with Ashtakvarga from Moon and Lagna, in judging the results of transit.

What Classical books say?

In considering whether a transit is good or bad, the position of planets from Moon at the time of birth is taken into consideration. Mantreswar states in book "Phaladeepika", that among all the Lagnas the moon's Lagna is the most important for assessing the effects of transit and is called the radical sign of Moon, which is also known as Chandra Lagna, or sometime as Janam Rashi. In the Indira Gandhi's horoscope, the Lagna or rising sign is Cancer, while Janam Rashi is Capricorn as Moon is located there.

Good Position for transit of Planets with respect to radical Moon

During the transit, all planets give good effects in 11th house. Sun, Rahu and Ketu give good result in 3rd, 6th, 10th houses. Mars and Saturn in 3rd and 6th houses. Moon in 1st, 3rd, 6th and 7th houses. Venus in all houses other than 6th, 7th and 10th houses. Jupiter in 2nd, 5th, 7th, 9th houses. Whereas Mercury in 2nd, 4th, 6th, 8th and 10th houses. When a planet transits through a sign whether favorable or not, if there is another planet moving at the same time in Vedha house, (Obstruction House), the effects of transit will not be felt. Following are the benefic and Vedha houses for each planet. Suppose Sun is transiting over 3rd house, it bound to give good results, but if at the same time if any planet is transiting in Vedha house then no good effects would be produced. It may be noted that there is no Vedha between Sun and Saturn, as Sun is father of Saturn. Similarly there is no Vedha between Moon and Mercury, as Moon is father of Mercury.

Sun gives good result in houses and No Vedha from Saturn

House	3	6	10	11
Vedha	9	12	4	5

Moon gives good result in houses. No Vedha from Mercury

House	1	3	6	7	10	11
Vedha	5	9	12	2	4	8

Mars gives good result in houses

House	3	6	11
Vedha	12	9	5

Mercury gives good result in houses. No Vedha from Moon

House	2	4	6	8	10	11
Vedha	5	3	9	1	7	12

Jupiter gives good result in houses

House	2	5	7	9	11
Vedha	12	4	3	10	8

Venus gives good result in houses

House	1	2	3	4	5	8	9	11	12
Vedha	8	7	1	10	9	5	11	6	3

Saturn gives good result in houses. No Vedha from Sun

House	3	6	11
Vedha	12	9	5

Rahu & Ketu gives good results in 3rd, 6th, 10th, 11th houses.

1. Vedha is only applicable to benefic house and not malefic house.

2. The above views are expressed in Narada Purana and Phaldeepika of Mantreshwara

Jatak Parijata is another book which says that each house has Vedha house if any planet transit in it.

Rashi	I	II	III	IV	V	VI	VII	VIII	IX	X	XI	XII
Sun	1	2	9	3	6	12	7	8	10	4	5	11
Moon	5	1	9	3	6	12	2	7	10	4	5	11
Mars	1	2	12	3	4	9	6	7	8	10	5	11
Mercury	2	5	4	3	7	9	6	7	8	8	12	11
Jupiter	1	12	2	5	4	6	3	7	10	9	8	11
Venus	8	7	1	10	9	12	2	5	11	4	3	6
Saturn	1	2	12	3	4	9	6	7	8	10	5	11

Meaning of above transit in different house in the light of Ashtakvarga.

It is stated that each planet has maximum 8 units, minimum 0 unit strength and 4 is middle point in Bhinnashtakvarga (BAV) and 56 units in Sarvashtakvarga (SAV) and middle point is 28.

General principles and results for 0 to 8 Bindus in Bhinnashtakvarga of Planets:-

0 – No shows Fear of death or great suffering

1 – No shows Losses, Destructions, worries, sickness

2 – No shows losses, Expenses, Obstruction in work/life.

3 – No shows Worries, Misunderstanding, Displeasure.

4 – No shows Mixed type results depending of Dasha.

5 – No shows health, wealth, good understanding with all.

6 – No shows Increase in wealth, Gain, high status.

7 – No shows All kind of happiness.

8 – No shows Fulfillments of all kind of desires, Fame in the Society

Good and bad results of Planets

1. **Sun:** If Sun is strong with Bindus then it will give results due to lordship of a particular house like victory over enemies, high status in Govt., health and wealth.

    Whereas weak Sun with less Bindu give unhappiness, obstacles, aimless traveling, separation from family, and displeasure from Govt., etc.

    Disease of Sun: headache, heart disease, chest ache, eye disease, stomach ache,

2. **Moon:** If strong with Bindus then it will gives wealth, good food, bed room comforts, clothing, friendship, association with opposite sex, joy, happiness, prosperity, good health.

    Moon with less Bindus gives weak mind, fear, all short of trouble, loss of health and wealth, disturbance of peace of mind, domestic unhappiness, laziness and jealousy.

    Disease of Moon: lungs, asthma, cholera, diarrhea, lunacy digestive disorders, jaundice, impurity of blood etc.

3. **Mars:** with strong Bindus give authority, success over enemies, victory, land, wealth, etc. and with less Bindus, it gives quarrels with sibling, exchange of hot words, loss of wealth / position, misunderstanding with wife, accidents.

    Disease of Mars: blood pressure, ulcers, cuts, bilious fever, impurity of blood.

4. **Mercury:** good speaking ability, wealth, prosperity, honour, good character, happiness.

    Weak Mercury gives loss of wealth, wicked speech, dishonour, grief, loss of position, dull intellect.

    Disease of Mercury: nervous disorder, brain, skin, anemia.

5. **Jupiter:** with strong Bindus in transits wealth, prosperity, birth of child, royal favour, association with noble persons, domestic

happiness, knowledge, land house, marriage.

With weak Bindu transits: loss of wealth, disgrace, loss of position, change of place, expenditure. Diseases are separation, liver, cancer, jaundice, diabetes.

6. **Venus transit with many Bindus:** luxury, perfumes, dress, enjoyments, marriage, children, wealth, prosperity, domestic happiness, pleasure trips, fame land, houses.

   Transit in weak Bindus house: debt, disgrace, litigation, losses, evils from woman, ill health to wife.

7. **Saturn transit in strong Bindus house:** wealth, servants land, pleasure, victory, permanent job, leader of masses, happy married life, honour.

   Whereas with weak Bindus house: it can gives ill health, death, journey to distance land, unnecessary hard work, separation from family / relatives, miseries, loss of wealth, obstruction, delay, imprisonment, calamities, grief.

   Disease of Saturn: chronic windy or phlegmatic type disease, rheumatism, dyspepsia, deformity.

A planet when transiting in a Rashi with more than 30 Bindus gives excellent results. Similarly, a planets transiting in a Rashi which in its own Bhinnashtakvarga has more than 4 Bindus gives auspicious results.

A planet while transiting a Rashi of its exaltation or own sign behaves good, whereas transiting in its debilitation sign is destructive. Saturn entered in Aries, a debilitation sign on April 17th, 1998. The result had been disastrous on a global scale. Fire, floods, earthquake wreaked havoc all around. Economies of South East Asia tumbled. Floods submerged the whole country of Bangladesh. NATO bombarded Yugoslavia on an unprecedented scale. The exodus of refugees from Kosovo reminded one of barbaric Middle Ages of murder, arson and loot. In India, the stability of the Govt. was threatened by withdrawal of support by

Jayalalitha, and vote for confidence in Govt. of Vajpayee was tabled on the floor of the house on April 15th, 1999 which BJP lost by one vote. There were other causes also – the entry of Venus, Lagna lord of horoscope of Independent India in Taurus/Gemini and its affliction which has been discussed in detail in my article in Journal of Astrology. Bhinnashtakvarga of Moon in the Independent horoscope of India, there is no Bindu in the sign of Gemini. Moon representing mind and 2nd house represent Family.

Transit through Nakshatras

Natal Star: The natal star is the Nakshatra in which Moon is located at the time of birth. In the horoscope of Indira Gandhi, the Moon is in Capricorn Rashi at 05^0 - $36^/$ - $48^{//}$ in Uttarashadha of Sun (number 21). This is his birth Nakshatra or natal star.

Phaldeepika has given in details, the results of transit of various planets in different Nakshatras. This view is at variance with that given by other authorities. According to them the transit of planets in 3rd, 5th, and 7th Nakshatra from the birth Nakshatra and their trines (12th and 21st; 14th and 23rd; 16th and 25th) cause misery in life. The 3rd and its trines called as Vipat Tara, whereas 5th and its trines are known as Pratihari and 7th and its Trines are called as Vedha Tara. When any benefic planet transit in these Nakshatras, the result are not good and when any malefic planet move over these Nakshatra, the results are very bad, especially when these planets are associated or aspected by malefic or in retrograde motion or combust.

The results of transit of various planets, as given in various classical works are as follows:-

Sun is malefic in 1st and 14th to 23rd Nakshatras from birth Nakshatra and it is good in rest of Nakshatras.

Moon is malefic in 1st, 2nd, 16th, 17th and 18th from birth Nakshatras and others are benefices.

Mars is malefic in 1st to 8th; 12th to 15th and 18th to 21st and rest is good.

Mercury, Jupiter and Venus is malefic in 1st to 3rd; 7th to 12th, 18th and 19th and rest is benefice Nakshatras

Saturn, Rahu and Ketu is malefic in 1st, 9th to 11th, 26th and 27th. Rest of Nakshatras is benefic.

Transit in Kakshaya: This is an important concept in Ashtakvarga and because of its importance has been dealt in a separate chapter.

Temporal Benefic and malefic for different Lagna:

While judging the results of transit of a planet its lordship must be kept in mind whether it is benefic or malefic for a particular Lagna as stated by Maharishi Parashara in Brihat Parashara Hora Shastra.

1.   Lagna lord is benefic i.e. Mars for Aries and Scorpio Lagna Saturn for Capricorn and Aquarius.

2.   Lord of 5th and 9th houses is always auspicious.

3.   Mars for cancer and Leo Lagna, Saturn for Taurus and Libra Lagna, Venus for Capricorn and Aquarius Lagna are Yogkarka being lords of Kendra and Trikona.

4.   Malefic lords of Kendra cease their malefic nature whereas benefic lords of Kendra have Kendraadhipati Dosha and do not give benefic results.

Aspects

The aspects during transit are also important. Benefic aspects on transiting planets give good results, while malefic aspects may prove disastrous.

Retrograde Planets

Useful table for Time of Ret rogation of Planets

Planets	Distance from Sun when started Retrogade	Distance from Sun when Become Direct	Nos of days of stationary before / after Retrograde	Total nos of days remain in Retrograde	Nos of days when Planet again become Retrogade
Saturn	251°	109°	5 Days	140 Days	378.1 Days
Jupiter	245°	115°	5 Days	120 Days	398.9 Days
Mars	228°	132°	3 Days	80 Days	779.9 Days
Venus	29°	29°	2 Days	42 Days	583.9 Days
Mercury	14° to 20°	17° to 20°	1 Day	24 Days	115.9 Days

A natural benefic in retrograde motion in transiting in favorable house enhances the signification of the house, while transiting in unfavorable house; the results will be less destructive.

A natural malefic in retrograde motion becomes destructive. If it is transiting through a 3rd, 6th or 11th house, its good effects are decreased. If it is transiting in good house i.e. Kendra or Trikona then its results are more malefic.

Dasha in Operation

1. Dasha of benefic planet while in transiting passing through a favorable house gives benefic effects to the maximum. In evil houses the benefic effects are reduced.

2. Dasha and transit of malefic in malefic house make the results worse. Whereas the transit through benefic house reduce the harmful effects.

Effect of Combustion

Planets when transiting through favorable position from Moon if become combust or get eclipsed by Rahu/Ketu can not give good results, whereas they give bad results in transit through unfavorable houses in similar circumstances.

The planets get combust in their nearness to Sun with in certain specified degrees.

The Moon gets combust if it is within	12^0 from Sun
The Mars gets combust if it is within	17^0 from Sun
The Mercury gets combust if it is within	14^0 from Sun
The Jupiter gets combust if it is within	11^0 from Sun
The Venus gets combust if it is within	10^0 from Sun
The Saturn gets combust if it is within	15^0 from Sun

Papkartri Yoga and Shubhkartri Yoga

If a planet, while transiting, gets hemmed in two malefic called 'Papkartri Yoga', its good effects are diluted in favorable houses and unfavorable houses its evils effects get accentuated. Whereas in Shubhkartri Yoga, the results are opposite

1) While transiting, the position of other planets should also be taken into account. The placement of benefic planets in 4th, 8th and 12th from its position is good, whereas malefic planets cause evils. These rules are similar to what have been prescribed by Parashara in judgment of Dasha/Antardasha.

2) Sun and Mars give their results in 1st Dreskona, Jupiter and Venus in 2nd Dreskona. Moon and Saturn in 3rd Dreskona. While Mercury and Rahu produce result through out the sign. The two and half year results should be judge from Saturn, the yearly results from Jupiter, the monthly from other inner planets and daily result from Moon.

3.   When a planet whose sub-period is in operation should happen to pass through its debilitation sign/Bhava, there will be misery or will not get good result. Same way in exaltation sign, it will give good result.

4.   Phaladeepika, a respected old treatise on Hindu Astrology has propounded the principles that for assessment of transit result, the placement of each planet in the birth horoscope be treated as Lagans and results of various houses assessed accordingly. This will be clear from the following example.

Suppose Venus is transiting in Taurus, treat Taurus as Lagna and predict the result according. The Scorpio is 7th house from Taurus and if there is no Bindu, the Mars is transiting over this sign; it will create marriage related problems. Similarly if there is 6 Bindus in 5th house from Taurus (Virgo) the transit of Mars over this house will give excellent results with regard to signification of this house i.e. Children, education, romance, etc.

Timing result of transit

According to Phaladeepika, the good or bad results will occur only when a planet cross the degree of its longitude in the birth chart. For example if in the birth chart Jupiter is at 15° in Aries and it is transiting in Scorpio having 8 Bindus, then the good results of this house will be forth coming only when Jupiter reaches 15°.

The effect of the house will be promoted even when a malefic occupies his own house. If a planet be in his sign of debilitation or in his enemy's house, the house occupied will be damaged.

If a benefic happens to own a Dusthana 3rd, 6th, 8th or 12th, it will destroy the house occupied by him even when he may be in his sign of exaltation. A malefic in exaltation will do good to the house occupied by him if it owns a good house - "Phaladeepika".

Chapter 16

Transit of Planets in Kakshaya

As there are 7 planets and Lagna (total eight), and Ashtakvarga deals with 8 types of energies, so each Rashi of 30° is divided into 8 parts of 3° 45'. These parts are known as Kakshaya. Each Kakshaya has its own lord in the following order.

No	Extent in Rashi	Name of the Lord	Period stays in
1.	0° to 3° 45'	Saturn	112 days
2.	3° 45' to 7° 30'	Jupiter	45 days
3.	7° 30 ' to 11° 15'	Mars	7 days
4.	11° 15' to 15°	Sun	3.8 days
5.	15° to 18° 45'	Venus	2.3 days
6.	18° 45 to 22° 30'	Mercury	22 hours
7.	22° 30 to 26° 15'	Moon	6.9 hrs.
8.	26° 15 to 30°	Lagna	

Lordship of Kakshaya has been allotted on the basis of distance from earth. Farthest planet is Saturn and nearest to earth is Moon.

Each planet when it enters a Rashi, first enters Kakshaya of Saturn then Jupiter, then Mars, Sun and so on. The last one being Kakshaya of Lagna. In ephemeris longitude of planets is given. Hence it is easy to find in which Kakshaya it is.

Saturn being the slowest planet (it stays in a Rashi for two and a half years) stays in a Kakshaya for 112 days, Jupiter 45 days, Mars 7 days, Sun 3.8 days, Venus 2.3 days, Mercury 22 hours and Moon 6.9 hours.

When a planet transits in a Rashi whose lord has contributed a Bindu, the result given are good irrespective of the fact whether a planet gives good or evil results as per normal transit rules. The fact whether a planet has contributed a Bindu or not is known from the chart of Prasthara Ashtakvarga of each planet as worked out in case of horoscope of Indira Gandhi.

Rules for Interpretation:

1. A planet transiting in a Kakshaya whose lord has contributed a Bindu gives benefic results. In case many planets are transiting in the same Kakshaya simultaneously results are bound to be better.

2. If however planets are transiting in a Binduless Kakshaya results are bound to be evil.

3. A planet transiting in a sign in which it has contributed a Bindu gives much wealth.

4. A planet transiting in a sign gives results because of its lordship, its signification as also signification of lord of the Kakshaya who has contributed a Bindu, over which a planet is transiting.

5. If the transiting planet and Kakshaya lords are friends results would be good.

6. In Ashtakvarga there is no exaltation or debilitation point, it is only the number of benefic Bindus contributed to a Rashi. Hence when analysing transits, all the corresponding Bhinnashtakvargas of planets present or connected with a particular Bhava has to be taken into consideration.

Chapter 17

Indu Lagna and
Wealth through Ashtakvarga

Ancient Books on Hindu Astrology mention frequently the word *Indu Lagna* or *Dhana Lagna*. It is also called *Visesha Chandra Yoga* by Parashara. Indu means Moon, and this special Lagna is made use of in assessing the level of wealth. However, experience has shown that this Lagna can also be used for predicting happy events of life and acquisition of property etc.

How to calculate Indu Lagna

Seven planets excluding (Rahu/Ketu) have been allotted *Kalas/* units as follows:

(a)	Sun	30
(b)	Moon	16
(c)	Mars	6
(d)	Mercury	8
(e)	Jupiter	10
(f)	Venus	12
(g)	Saturn	1

1. Add *Kalas* allotted to lord of nine from Lagna as well as Moon.

2. Expunge multiples of 12 and get the remainder. If the remainder is 0 make it 12.

3.   Count from Moon (that is why it is called Indu) as many houses as the remainder is.

4.   This particular house so arrived at is known as 'Indu Lagna'.

Example:

(i)   In the horoscope of Queen Elizabeth, lord of 9 from Lagna is Mercury. It has been allotted 8 Kalas. The lord of nine from Moon is Jupiter who gets 10 Kalas. Add 8 and 10 together, and you get 18 Kalas.

(ii)   Divide 18 by 12 and you get a remainder of 6.

(iii)   Count 6 from Moon. This is Sagittarius, the 12th house which in this particular horoscope is Indu Lagna.

Some of the astrologers use Jaimini system for computing Indu Lagna, and make use of Jaimini aspects. In this Kalas (rays) or units are the same. But the method of counting nine is different in odd and even signs. If Lagna / Moon are in the odd signs counting is direct, if in even signs counting is indirect. Aspects used are Jaimini and not Parashari. In Jaimini system, movable Rashis (Aries, Cancer, Libra and Capricorn) aspect fixed Rashis (Taurus, Leo, Scorpio and Aquarius) excepting adjacent ones and vice versa. The dual Rashis (Gemini, Virgo, Sagittarius and Pisces) aspect one another. The aspects of Rashis include planets in it.

Mer	Sun		Rah
Ven	Queen Elizabeth 21-4-1926		Mon
Lag Jup Mar			
Indu Lagna Ket	Sat		

The more planets aspect Indu Lagna, the better are the results for wealth.

Example:

In the above horoscope, Lagna is even sign so the counting would start in the reverse direction from Lagna. Counting nine in this way from Lagna, you get sign Taurus whose lord is Venus. Venus gets 12 Kalas.

Moon is also in even sign, so counting would be again in reverse direction. Nine counting in this way brings us to Scorpio, whose lord is Mars. Mars gets 6 Kalas. Add 12 and 6 we get 18. Divide 18 by 12 and you get a remainder of 6. Since Moon is in the even sign counting 6 in reverse direction brings us to Aquarius which is Indu Lagna as per Jaimini rule. Aquarius is fixed sign. It has the aspect of Aries, which has exalted Sun, and Cancer having Moon. The sign Capricorn being adjacent to Aquarius does not aspect it. Two powerful luminaries aspect Indu Lagna.

How to interpret Indu Lagna

Combination for immense Riches

(i)   Indu Lagna occupied or aspected by many benefic planets give lot of wealth in their Dasha. Even aspect of one benefic is good for this purpose. This is known as *Koteeshwar Yoga.*

(ii) Exalted malefic (Saturn, Sun and Mars) planets in Indu Lagna give immense riches towards the end - *Koteeshwar Yoga.* Even malefics in this Lagna give wealth, though not so much.

(iii) Even one benefic planet aspected by benefic or malefic gives plenty of wealth.

(iv) Occupied by pure malefics it gives moderate wealth.

(v)   All planets situated in it or aspecting this Lagna give wealth during their Dashas.

(vi) Also planets situated in trines or quadrants (Trikona and Kendras), **from this Lagna** gives **wealth during their** Dasha/Antardashas.

(vii) It has been observed that Jupiter in transit, when it comes in Kendras from this Lagna, gives property, wealth and happiness.

(viii) The planets situated in 3, 6, 8 and 12 from this Lagna destroy wealth.

(ix) Indu Lagna aspected by debilitated malefic is not good for finances. Similarly, Indu Lagna neither aspected nor occupied by planets is not good.

(x) While making a judgment of Indu Lagna see the condition of 2nd and 11th house/lord from this Lagna. This will give a good idea of the level of prosperity.

(xi) Treating Indu Lagna as the first house form an estimate of Dhana Yogas, which are formed by the combinations of 2nd, 5th, 9th, 11th and 10th houses/lords.

(xii) Use of Sarvashtakvarga may be made effectively in determining the strength of the relevant houses/lords.

Examples:

Bill Gates

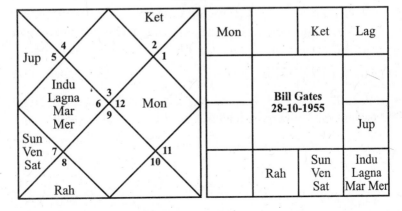

In the horoscope of Bill Gates, the richest man in the world today, Lagna is Gemini

The 9th from this sign is Aquarius whose lord is Saturn, who is allotted 1 Kala. The 9th from Moon is Scorpio; its lord gets 6 units. 6 + 1 = 7. The 7th from Moon is sign Virgo which is Indu Lagna. It has 2 planets, exalted Lagna and 4th lord Mercury, and lord of 6th and 11th Mars. The second from it is very powerful and has 3 planets, lord of 5th in 5, exalted Saturn and Sun having Neechbhanga Raj Yoga. 11th from Indu Lagna it is sign Cancer whose lord Moon is again aspecting Indu Lagna from a most powerful Kendra 10th house.

K. K. Birla

Mer Rah　8 Mar　9	Sun Ven　7	6 5	Sat
Mon　10	4 1		
11 12	Indu Lagna	3 2	Jup
	Ket		

	Indu Lagna	Ket	Jup
	K.K. Birla **11-11-1918**		Sat
Mon			
Mar	Mer Rah	Lag Sun Ven	

In the horoscope of K. K. Birla, Lagna is Libra. 9th from it is Gemini, whose lord Mercury has 8 *Kalas*. The 9th from Moon is again Mercury having 8 *Kalas*. 8 + 8 = 16. Sixteen divided by 12 leaves a remainder of 4. The 4th from Moon is Aries, which is Indu Lagna for our purpose. This Lagna is aspected by Lagna lord Venus from its Mool Trikona sign and Sun having Neechbhanga Raj Yoga. Moon is in Kendra from this Lagna, and two planets, Yogakaraka Saturn and Mars are in Trikonas from this Indu Lagna. In the Sarvashtak, all the important wealth giving houses, Lagna, 2nd, 4th, 9th, 10th, and 11th are strong, having 30, 29, 30, 28, 27, and 35 Bindus. (See rule in earlier chapter on financial prosperity).

Mukesh Ambani

Indu Lagna	Lag Sun Ven Mer Ket	Mar	
	Mukesh Ambani		
			Jup
Mon	Sat	Rah	

In this horoscope Lagna is Aries. The 9th lord is Jupiter having 10 Kalas.

The 9th lord from Moon is Sun, with 30 Kalas. 10 + 30 = 40. Dividing 40 by 12 we get a remainder of 4. The 4th house from Moon is Pisces, which is Indu Lagna. 2nd from this Lagna is very powerful house with exalted 5th lord Sun, 2nd lord Venus, 3rd and 6th lord Mercury, with Ketu (treating Ketu as Mars in powerful Aries.) Lord of Indu Lagna, Jupiter is in powerful Trikona aspected by Lagna lord Mars.

26	22 Lag	26	34
44	Mukesh Ambani		26
34			26
25	22	20	32

In the Sarvashtakchakra, 10th and 11th house are very powerful with 34 and 44 Bindus, eleven house having more Bindus than tenth and 12th having less Bindus than eleven. This is a formidable combination for prosperity.

Use of Indu Lagna through Ashtakvarga

Use of Sarvashtakvarga may be made effectively in determining the strength of the relevant houses/lords.

Treating Lagna as the first house to an estimate of Dhana Yogas, which are formed by the combinations of 2nd, 5th, 9th, 10th and 11th house/lords.

While making a judgement of Indu Lagna see the condition of 2nd and 11th house/lord from this lagna. This will give a good idea of the level of prosperity through Sarvashtakvargas.

1.   If Lagna, nine, ten and eleven houses have 30 Bindus or more person will be rich from birth to death.

2.   If Lagna and fourth houses having 33 points and its lords has exchanged the house than native will be wealthy.

3.   If 11th house has more Bindus than the 10th house and 12th house have fewer Bindus than the 11th house it is good for wealth. Moreover, if Lagna has more Bindus than the 12th house the native enjoys all the material comforts of life

4.   The native will be beggar if the Lagna, 9th, 10th, 11th houses are having less than 25 points in each house and malefic are in trine houses (1, 5 and 9).

5.   According to some classical books if the total Bindus of Lagna + 2 + 4 + 9 + 10 + 11 houses are more than 164, then native is wealthy. In the same way add the Bindus of 6 + 8 + 12 houses. If they are less than 76 then the income will be more than the expenditure.

This may not come true in modern times. It is been observed that the 6th house stands for competition or to fight back to regain some things lost. 8th house represents black money as also inherited property, lottery, unearned income or sudden gain from shares etc., 12th house stands for gain from foreign country or multinational company.

6.   If 2nd house has more points from 12th house then native is hardly spending any money for his enjoyment. He may be hoarding up his money in a bank or so.

7.   If 12th house has more points than 11th house than it means (1) More expenses than earning, this means taking loans, etc. (2) earning from foreign sources or country or working in Multi-nation company. (A native goes out of country only if his 4th house and its lord are afflicted and has PAC with 12th house or its lord).

Chapter 18

Longevity

Numerous methods have been given in ancient classical books for determination of longevity. The best results are, however, obtained through Parashari Dasha scheme supplemented with Jaimini system.

Calculation of age on the basis of Ashtakvarga alone may not give accurate results. While in Ashtakvarga also many methods are given, we are mentioning here just two which generally popular.

1. Nakshatraayus System – Based on Sarvashtakvarga

Step No, 1

Make the Sarvashtakvarga of the horoscope and calculate the Shodhya Pinda as detailed in earlier chapters.

Rajiv Gandhi's Horoscope taken as Example:-

26	28	31	50
19			23
35			Lag 23
26	23	31	22

Graha Pinda of Sarvashtakvarga

Planets	Sun	Moon	Mars	Mercury	Jupiter	Venus	Saturn	Total
Pinda	45	45	24	45	90	63	0	312

Rashi Pinda of Sarvashtakvarga

Rashi	1	2	3	4	5	6	7	8	9	10	11	12	Total
Pinda	14	0	0	36	90	15	35	16	0	20	44	0	270

Total Graha Pinda and Rashi Pinda

= 312 + 270 = Shodhya Pinda =   582

Multiply Shodhya Pinda by 7 and divide by 27 i.e.

582 x 7 = 4074 -:- 27 = 150.8 will be Nakshatra years age which convert into Solar years i.e. 150.8 x 324 -:- 365.25 = 134 approx

If quotient is more than 100 then detect it from 100, if it is less than 100 then retain it as it is. We get figure 134 and have to reduce 100 and balance is 34 years age.

This is called the Nakshatrayush of the native.

Method II — Based on Bhinnashtakvarga

Work out Shodhya Pinda of each planet as detailed in earlier chapters. This involves following steps:-

1. Make Bhinnashtakvarga of all seven planets i.e. Sun, Moon, Mars, Mercury, Jupiter, Venus and Saturn.

2. Make reduction I and reduction II - Trikona and Ekadhipatya reductions

3. Get Graha and Rashi Pinda, add both of them to get Shodhya Pinda of each planet.

4. In short we get following Shodhya Pindas for each planet

Planet	Sun	Moon	Mars	Mercury	Jupiter	Venus	Saturn
Shodhya Pinda	145	170	152	192	160	122	256

Longevity contributed by each planet:

Multiply the Shodhya Pinda of each planet by 7 and divide the product by 27. Obtain the quotient. If it is more than 27, reduce it from 27 and take the balance. It is said that no planet can give more than 27 years gross age and it has to be less then 27 years. (As given in Shambu Hora Prakash) This is the gross years of longevity contributed by each planet, the contribution made by each planet are as follows

Planet	Shodhya Pinda	Multiply by	Product got	Divide by 27	Quotient got	Reducing 27	Gross age
Sun	145	7	1015	27	37	-27	10
Moon	170	7	1190	27	44	-27	17
Mars	152	7	1064	27	39	-27	12
Mercury	192	7	1344	27	49	-27	22
Jupiter	160	7	1120	27	41	-27	14
Venus	122	7	854	27	31	-27	04
Saturn	256	7	1792	27	66	-27&-27	12

Reduction or Haranas

The gross yeas arrived at above are subject to further reduce by following principles:-

Reduction by one half

A) If there are more planets than one in a Rashi its term of life should be reduced by half. There are 5 planets in Lagna in Rajiv's horoscope, so all will get half of the given gross age.

B) If a planet is debilitated or combustion, one half is be deducted. As case of Jupiter

Reduction by one third

a) If planet is in sign of enemy (as the case of Mars and Venus), hence a reduction of 1/3 has to be reduce.

b) If a planet suffers defeat in Graha Yudda (planetary war)

c) If Sun and Moon are with Rahu and Ketu i.e. at the time of eclipsed

Reduction in Visible half of the horoscope, then do the following reduction.

S.No.	If Planets in	If Malefic then reduce	If Benefic then reduce
1	The 12 house	Full	1/2
2	The 11 house	1/2	1/4
3	The 10 house	1/3	1/6
4	The 9 house	1/4	1/8
5	The 8 house	1/5	1/10
6	The 7 house	1/6	1/12

When same planet is subject to many reductions, only highest reduction should be taken.

Applying these reduction to given above horoscope.

Gross Age given by planet		1/2 reduction		1/3 reduction			Visible half reduction	Net age
		A	B	a	b	c		
Sun	10	5	X	X	X	X	X	5
Moon	17	8. 5	X	X	X	X	X	8. 5
Mars	12	X	X	8	X	X	X	8
Mercury	22	11	X	X	X	X	X	11
Jupiter	14	7	7	X	X	X	X	7
Venus	04	2	X	2.8 Mts	X	X	X	2.8
Saturn	12	X	X	X	X	X	6	6

Add net years together = 48 Yrs 2 Mts

This is Nakshatra years age which has to convert to solar years as the same way as we did above. i.e. 48 x 324 -:- 365.25 = 42.5 years we get net age of longevity, whereas Rajiv Gandhi lived for about 47 years.

Note:- as said earlier this method is totally not accurate by using different methods to numbers of horoscopes, mostly being at variance from the actual life term enjoyed by the native. It is due to numbers of controversies involved in it. Some says if Saturn is strong in the chart then use Sarvashtakvarga method and if Mars is strong then use Bhinnashtakvarga method. There are some others who say different things.

Hence the methods used here for calculating at the basis of Ashtakvarga cannot be applied to every horoscope. The methods are described here with examples just to understand the methods. Research works alone can give us clue to find out the defects in this system.

Chapter 19

Results of Dasha / Antardasha

The Dasha that we are using here is Vimshottari Dasha and not the Ashtakvarga Dasha.

Condition of the Dasha Lord

1. First apply the basic principles of astrology: the Dasha lord gives good results if it is exalted, located in its own house, has lord ship of Lagna, 5th or 9th house, and is not aspected or associated with malefics. The benefic planets give best results while placed in Kendra or Trikona, while malefics are good if placed in 3, 6, or 11.

2. A debilitated, or combust planet, or having lordship of 6, 8 or 12 or ill placed therein does not normally give good results and creates much evil.

3. A malefic planet aspected / associated with benefics improves its position, whereas benefic planet having aspect association of malefic gives mixed results.

4. Dasha of the Lagna lord, 10th lord and of an exalted planet is the best Dasha in life. Results will again depend upon the condition of the dash lord.

5. In case a planet is lord of a good as well as a bad house, then in that case see where his Mooltrikona sign is located. If Mooltrikona sign is in Dusthana house i.e. in 3, 6, 8, or 12, then evil results will predominate otherwise good results will

prevail. For example Saturn of Virgo Lagna is both lord of 5th and 6th. But since his Mooltrikona sign is in 6th, evil results will be more. As 5th lord he will give good education to the native, but since he is also 6th lord the attainment of educational status may not be very high.

6.   A Dasha lord will not only gives the results of the houses he owns/aspects but will also give the results because of his Karkatwas (significations). For example Jupiter as lord of 7 and 10 in Gemini Lagna will give results of 7th house, partnership, marriage etc. , as lord of 10th profession and fame but also as he is Karka for children, wealth and knowledge all these things would be visible. Since he has also Kendra Adhipatya Dosha, the effects of these should also be taken into consideration.

7.   Malefic should not be placed in 4, 8, 5 or 9th from the Dasha lord. It should not be in Papkartari Yoga.

8.   The planets placed in 3, 6, 10, and 11, the Upchhaya houses give gradually good results.

9.   The placement of the planet both from Lagna as well as Moon should be seen to decide lord ship. For example in the horoscope of Indira Gandhi, Jupiter is lord of 6th and 9th houses from Lagna whereas he is lord of 3rd and 12th from Moon.

10.   Ashtakvarga is a great help in giving judgement about results of the Dasha/Antar. If Dasha lord contains more than 4 Bindus in the Rashi located, as well the Rashi in which it is placed has more than 28 Bindus the overall effects of the Dasha would be good.

11.   Similarly, if there is a Bindu in the Kakshaya, contributed by the Kakshaya lord, where Dasha lord is located, the results would be favourable.

Antardasha or Sub-period

Similarly the condition of Antardasha lord should be ascertained. To enable it to give good results it should not be located in

i) 1, 6, 8 or 12 from the Dasha lord

ii) It should not be combust or debilitated.

Chapter 20

Muhurta and Ashtakvarga

Muhurta and Sun

1. Auspicious Month - When Sun is transiting in a Rashi having 5 or more Bindus in its Ashtakvarga, it is good time for performance of:-

    i)   Marriage, religious, charitable and other auspicious ceremonies,

    ii) Journey to distant place or pilgrimage,

    iii) Starting new ventures.

2. Deity of Shiva should be installed in the direction indicated by a sign, which has maximum Bindus in Ashtakvarga of Sun.

    Direction can also be obtained by adding the total number of Bindus in the three Trikona Rashis representing a particular direction. For example Aries, Leo and Sagittarius Rashis represent Eastern direction, signs Taurus, Virgo and Capricorn represent Southern direction, the signs Gemini, Libra and Aquarius represent Western direction while signs Cancer, Scorpio and Pisces represent Northern direction. Add the total in each group. Choose the direction, which is represented by the group, which has maximum Bindus in Sun's Ashtakvarga for all auspicious functions and service with the government as well as worship of deities.

    A native should take loan or medicine, when rising sign of the day is having less point in Sarvashtakvarga of his horoscope and then the next sign is having more Bindus so as to be able to return the loan or have a fast recovery.

Part of the Day for Auspicious Work:

1st part of the day is indicated by the house where Sun is located in the horoscope and three subsequent houses.

2nd part of the day is represented by the 5th, 6th, 7th and 8th house from position of the Sun.

3rd part of the day represented by 9th to 12th houses from location of the Sun.

One should start for auspicious work during that part of the day which part is strong in Bhinnashtakvarga of Sun.

Location of Kitchen:

In Mars Bhinnashtakvarga, add Bindus of 1, 5, 9; 2, 6, 10; 3, 7, 11; and 4, 8, 12; whichever group of Rashis has got the maximum number, the kitchen of the native if placed in that direction would give him good food, which will keep the native disease free, thus assuring longevity.

Purchase of Land and Property: The best time to buy land or property is when Mars is transiting in a sign having maximum number of Bindus in its own Ashtakvarga

Ashtakvarga of Moon and Muhurta

1. Ceremonies like tonsure and betrothal should be done when Moon is passing through a sign having maximum Bindus.

2. For a good Muhurta for any event Moon should be transiting in Rashis with 5 or more than five Bindus and Moon should be strong.

3. In Moon's Bhinnashtakvarga, Bindus contribution made by 1, 5, 9 Rashis or; 2, 6, 10 Rashis or 3, 7, 11 Rashis or 4, 8, 12 Rashis whichever is strongest or has the highest total, in that direction one's bathroom should be situated. These are Kaala

Purusha Bhavas in which 1, 5, 9 signifies East; 2, 6, 10 signifies South; 3, 7, 11 signifies West; and 4, 8, 12 signifies North.

Ashtakvarga of Mercury and Muhurta

1. In Mercury's Ashtakvarga find out signs having more than 4 Bindus and aspected by Jupiter. Education should be started at the time when Mercury is transiting over such a sign.

2. Propitiation should be done to Vishnu, at the time when sign with maximum Bindus in Ashtakvarga of Mercury is rising

Auspicious Time for *Japas* etc.

When Sun transits signs having high number of Bindus in the Ashtakvarga of Jupiter, that is the time for performing auspicious ceremonies.

Also when Jupiter transits sign in which he has largest number of Bindus the time is auspicious for *Japas, Tapas,* prayers, initiation, performance of religious functions rituals, study of Vedas, feeding guests and Brahmins.

Agricultural Work:

The good time to recruit servants and start agricultural work, etc. is at the time when Saturn is transiting over a Bhava having maximum number of Bindus or that sign is rising during the day.

Location of Servant Quarters:

Servant quarters, places for store, toilets should be located in the direction represented by Rashi having highest number of Bindus in the Ashtakvarga of Saturn.

Chapter 21

Marriage and Ashtakvarga

Great use of Ashtakvarga can be made of in ensuring success in the married life. However normal astrological principles in ensuring a happy married life should not be ignored. For a happy married life following factors are necessary:

1. Lagna / Lagna lord and 7th lord should be strong. This has been discussed in details in the author's book Analyzing Horoscope through modern Techniques.

2. Venus should be well placed in the horoscope. It should not be debilitated, combust, in an enemy sign or in 6, 8 and 12.

3. It should not be in *Papkartari Yoga.*

4. Venus should not be afflicted by Mars, Rahu or Saturn. This destroys the harmony in married life.

5. Venus should not be in the beginning or end of the sign.

6. Darakarka and Uppada should be well placed.

7. Lagna lord and 7th lord should not be in 6, 8, or 12 from each other.

8. 2nd house of Kutumbha and 4th house of Sukhsthan should not be afflicted.

9. Affliction to Mars disturbs married life.

10. Saturn and Mercury, two impotent planets should not afflict 7th house / seventh lord.

In Ashtakvarga some more principles are stated in classical books.

Some rules given in the classical books about a happy married life are as follows

a)   Wife/ Husband should be from a direction represented by the sign having maximum number of Bindus in the Ashtakvarga of Venus. If the spouse comes from the direction represented by the Rashi having the maximum number of Bindus, in Venus Bhinnashtakvarga, the married life is a happy one.

b)   Husband and wife will love each other when in the 7th from Venus in his own Ashtakvarga a Bindu has been contributed by a planet that happens to own one's birth star or its trines. If Rahu and Ketu happen to be the rulers of birth Nakshatras, the planets Saturn and Mars should be substituted on the analogy Dictum *Sanivad* Rahu.

Unhappiness will result if wife/husband is from the direction having least number of Bindus.

Match Making

1)   Choose a partner whose Moon sign or Lagna corresponds to signs having maximum number of Bindus in native's horoscope.

2)   See in whose Kakshaya Moon of the native is posited. Supposing it is in the Kakshaya of Jupiter. Then choose a partner from one of those Moon signs in which Jupiter has contributed a Bindu.

Nehru's Moon is of degrees 17°-51' minute.

Hence it is in Kakshaya of Venus. In Moon Parstharachakra Venus has contributed Bindus in the signs, Aries, Gemini, Cancer, Leo, Sagittarius, Capricorn and Aquarius. Partner can be chosen who has Moon in any one of these signs.

Chapter 22

Controversies in Ashtakvarga

I. Trikona Shodhana:

The principle that has been followed in this book is as propounded by Parashara, according to which of the three triangular signs, the figure of the sign having least number of Bindus has to be deducted from the figures of all the signs and the remainder will represent rectified figures of the signs.

There is another view about reductions which is given by Balabhadra as given by him in his book Hora Ratnam, according to this view if the figures in three trinal signs are unequal then the figures of all the three should be equated to the least one.

For example in Moon's Ashtakvarga the Bindus in signs Aries, Leo and Sagittarius (1, 5, and 9) are 3, 2 and 5 respectively then instead of deducting 2 from all the three signs, you make Bindus in all the three signs equal to the least or 2 in this case.

According to Mantreswar of Phaladeepika the principles of reduction are as follows:

1. If the figures in the three trinal signs are unequal make all the three equal to the least one. (Like we have done above).

2. If there are no Bindus in two of the trinal signs, remove figures in the third.

3. When all the three signs have same number of Bindus, then remove them and make them 0 in all the three signs.

II. Bhava Chart Vs Rashi Chart

Suppose a person is born when the Ascendant rising is 3 degrees. Compare his fate with that of a person who is born after him more than one and half an hour in the same Ascendant at 27 degrees or so. They may have been born in the same Rashis but their fates would be different because of the concept of Bhava Madhya. The planets may be in the same Rashis but they may be in different Bhavas and hence would give different results.

1. Some of the authorities on Ashtakvarga are of the opinion that the Bhava chart is more important than the Rashi chart. A planet in a horoscope may be in a particular house in the Rashi chart but when a Bhava Chart is cast it might be in a different house because of the conception of Bhava Madhya. This use of Bhava Madhya was popularized by Sripathi. Because of this if a planet were in a different Bhava it would give different results. Therefore, it has been suggested that Ashtakvarga should be calculated on the basis of Bhava chart and not Rashi chart.

2. In general predictive astrology it is recognized that Bhava chart is as important as a Rashi chart. It is for this reason that both Rashi and Bhava chart are scrutinized for sound predictions.

3. Certain Yogas like Gaja Kesari Yogas are formed only on the basis of Bhavas, and not on basis of Rashis such as Gaja Kesari Yoga, which is formed when Moon and Jupiter are in Kendra from each other.

As against this the authorities that believe that it is Rashi that is more important have following things to say.

1. The proper place for a planet is a Rashi and not Bhava. It is on this basis that planets get exalted and debilitated at certain specified degrees.

2. All divisional charts, Navamsa, Dashamsa, Saptamsa etc. are cast on the basis of Rashis and degrees of Lagna planets.

3.   Jaimini astrology uses only Rashis and not Bhavas.

4.   Ownership of planets are based on the basis of Rashis only. For example Venus owns Rashis Taurus and Libra, while Jupiter is lord of Sagittarius and Pisces. For this purpose Bhavas do not come into the picture.

5.   The concept of Kakshaya divides Rashis into eight parts. For this purpose Bhavas do not come into the picture.

6.   Temporary friendship / enmity is based of Rashis alone.

7.   Trikona and Ekadhipatya reductions are done on the basis of Rashis alone.

8.   The laws relating to Rashi Gunakara are based on Rashis alone.

III. Bindus 337 or 386 – Lagan Ashtak

The total numbers of Bindus in Sarvashtakvarga are 337. Some authorities state that Bindus of Laganashtak, which are 49, should also be included to make it to 386. Their reasoning is as follows:

1.   Parashara has given the Ashtakvarga of Lagna also to make it ashtak (eight). He has allotted total of 49 Bindus for it.

2.   Lagna ashtak is essential factor for calculating longevity.

3.   While Lagna is fixed so its lord has effects in transit.

As Against this majority is of the opinion that only 337 Bindus should be used. Following reasons are assigned for this

1.   In the Bhinnashtak of different planets the auspicious places from Lagna have already been taken into consideration. There is no use adding this twice.

2.   Lagna is a fixed entity and has no transit.

3.   If Lagna ashtak is added the total of sarvashtak becomes 386, which divided by 12 give us a quotient of 32, but all authorities on Ashtakvarga use 28 Bindus as average strength for Rashis/ house.

Benefic places for Lagna from the planets

From Saturn	:	1 - 3 - 4 - 6 - 10 - 11	=	6
From Jupiter	:	1 - 2 - 4 - 5 - 6 - 7 - 9 - 10 - 11	=	9
From Mars	:	1 - 3 - 6 - 10 - 11	=	5
From Sun	:	3 - 4 - 6 - 10 - 11 - 12	=	6
From Venus	:	1 - 2 - 3 - 4 - 5 - 8 - 9	=	7
From Mercury	:	1 - 2 - 4 - 6 - 8 - 10 - 11	=	7
From Moon	:	3 - 6 - 10 - 11 - 12	=	5
From Lagna	:	3 - 6 - 10 - 11	=	4
		Total	=	**49**

IV. Rahu's Ashtakvarga:

Most of the ancient books on astrology ignore Rahu's Ashtakvarga. It is only Shambhu Hora Prakash which makes a mention of Rahu's Ashtakvarga. Most of the authorities agree that the total numbers of Bindus are 337. Since Rahu only a shadow planet, it has been excluded from the above scheme.

According to the book mentioned above the benefic position of Rahu with reference to other planets are as follows:

From Sun	:	1, 2, 3, 5, 7, 8 and 10
From Moon	:	1, 3, 5, 7, 8, 9 and 10
From Mars	:	2, 3, 5, ⑦ and 12
From Mercury	:	2, 4, 7, 8 and 12
From Jupiter	:	1, 3, 4, 6 and 8
From Venus	:	6, 7, 11 and 12
From Saturn	:	3, 5, 7, 10, 11 and 12
From Lagna	:	3, 4, 5, 9 and 12
Total	:	**43 / 44**

Note: **Dr. B. V. Raman has taken 44 points instead of 43 points, adding 7th place from Mars, where as other classical books like Phaladeepika, Shambhu Hora Prakash has taken only 43 points.**

1.   There is no benefic place of Rahu from Rahu himself, as it is only shadowy planet. Hence there is no need to do reduction I or II.

2.   While transit results of Rahu through other Kakshaya can be given in the normal way, no Kakshaya has been allotted to Rahu.

3.   The movement of Rahu is in reverse, therefore, the transit through Kakshaya would be as follows: Lagna, Moon, Mercury, Venus, Sun, Mars, Jupiter and Saturn. It stays in a Kakshaya for two and a quarter months.

4.   Result of Transit - Like other malefics the result or transit of Rahu in 3 - 6 - 10 & 11 from Moon are good. They are bad in other houses.

Chapter 23

Example Horoscopes

1 Horoscope of Independent India

DOB: 15-08-1947 TOB: 00-01-00 Hrs POB: New Delhi

		Lag Rah	Mar
			Sun Mer Sat Ven
	15-8-1947		
	Ket	Jup	

Bhinnashtakvarga

Planets	1	2	3	4	5	6	7	8	9	10	11	12
Sun	6	4	4	4	4	3	3	1	4	4	5	6
Moon	6	6	0	5	2	6	5	4	3	5	4	3
Mars	3	6	2	4	1	5	2	2	5	2	3	4
Mercury	4	7	4	4	5	4	4	3	5	2	5	7
Jupiter	5	6	4	4	6	4	4	6	5	5	2	6
Venus	3	8	4	4	5	5	4	5	2	1	6	5
Saturn	3	7	2	2	4	3	3	2	4	1	4	4
Total	30	44	19	27	27	30	25	23	28	20	29	35

After Trikona Shodhyan (Reduction)

Planets	1	2	3	4	5	6	7	8	9	10	11	12
Sun	2	1	1	3	0	0	0	0	0	1	2	5
Moon	4	1	0	2	0	1	5	1	1	0	4	0
Mars	2	4	0	2	0	3	0	0	4	0	1	2
Mercury	0	5	0	1	1	2	0	0	1	0	1	4
Jupiter	0	2	1	0	1	0	2	2	0	1	0	2
Venus	1	7	0	0	3	4	0	1	0	0	2	1
Saturn	0	6	0	0	1	2	1	0	1	0	2	2

After Ekadhipatya Shodhyan (Reduction)

Planets	1	2	3	4	5	6	7	8	9	10	11	12
Sun	2	1	1	3	0	0	0	0	0	1	1	5
Moon	1	1	0	2	0	1	5	1	1	0	4	0
Mars	2	4	0	2	0	3	0	0	2	0	1	2
Mercury	0	5	0	1	1	2	0	0	1	0	1	1
Jupiter	0	2	1	0	1	0	2	2	0	1	0	2
Venus	0	7	0	0	3	4	0	0	0	0	2	1
Saturn	0	6	0	0	1	3	1	0	1	0	2	1

Shodhya Pinda

Planets	Sun	Moon	Mars	Mercury	Jupiter	Venus	Saturn
Rashi Pinda	120	126	130	106	97	154	130
Graha Pinda	089	104	054	027	28	000	010
Total	209	230	184	133	125	154	140

2   Bill Clinton

DOB: 19-08-1946 TOB: 08-30-00 Hrs POB:

Bhinnashtakvarga

Planets	1	2	3	4	5	6	7	8	9	10	11	12
Sun	4	4	6	3	5	4	2	3	3	2	6	6
Moon	3	6	5	5	1	4	5	5	2	6	5	2
Mars	3	3	4	5	2	5	3	2	3	2	4	3
Mercury	6	6	4	7	2	6	4	3	5	4	3	4
Jupiter	4	6	5	5	4	4	7	4	6	3	4	4
Venus	4	7	4	6	3	4	3	6	4	3	4	4
Saturn	1	3	5	3	4	5	0	4	3	1	7	3
Total	25	35	33	34	21	32	24	27	26	21	33	26

After Trikona Shodhyan (Reduction)

Planets	1	2	3	4	5	6	7	8	9	10	11	12
Sun	1	2	4	0	2	2	0	0	0	0	4	3
Moon	2	2	0	3	0	0	0	3	1	2	0	0
Mars	1	1	1	3	0	3	0	0	1	0	1	1
Mercury	4	2	1	4	0	2	1	0	3	0	0	1
Jupiter	0	3	1	1	0	1	3	0	2	0	0	0
Venus	1	4	1	2	0	1	0	2	1	0	1	0
Saturn	0	2	5	0	3	4	0	1	2	0	7	0

After Ekadhipatya Shodhyan (Reduction)

Planets	1	2	3	4	5	6	7	8	9	10	11	12
Sun	1	2	2	0	2	2	0	0	0	0	4	3
Moon	2	2	0	3	0	0	0	2	1	2	0	0
Mars	1	1	0	3	0	3	0	0	0	0	1	0
Mercury	4	1	0	4	0	2	1	0	1	0	0	1
Jupiter	0	0	0	1	0	1	3	0	2	0	0	0
Venus	1	4	0	2	0	1	0	1	1	0	1	0
Saturn	0	2	4	0	3	4	0	1	2	0	7	0

Shodhya Pinda

Planets	Sun	Moon	Mars	Mercury	Jupiter	Venus	Saturn
Rashi Pinda	153	81	55	092	48	88	205
Graha Pinda	045	40	80	100	55	40	075
Total	**198**	**121**	**135**	**192**	**103**	**128**	**280**

3 George W. Bush

DOB: 06-07-1946 TOB: 07-46-00 Hrs POB: New Haven

Bhinnashtakvarga

Planets	1	2	3	4	5	6	7	8	9	10	11	12
Sun	5	5	6	4	2	4	2	3	4	4	5	4
Moon	6	5	3	3	2	7	3	5	5	4	2	4
Mars	3	5	3	4	3	3	2	4	3	1	5	3
Mercury	7	6	3	6	5	3	5	4	3	1	7	4
Jupiter	5	5	4	5	5	4	4	6	6	3	2	7
Venus	6	7	2	5	3	5	5	5	3	4	3	4
Saturn	3	5	4	5	1	3	2	2	6	3	3	2
Total	35	38	25	32	21	29	23	29	30	20	27	28

After Trikona Shodhyan (Reduction)

Planets	1	2	3	4	5	6	7	8	9	10	11	12
Sun	3	1	4	1	0	0	0	0	2	0	3	1
Moon	4	1	1	0	0	3	1	2	3	0	0	1
Mars	0	4	1	1	0	2	0	1	0	0	3	0
Mercury	4	5	0	2	2	2	2	0	0	0	4	0
Jupiter	0	2	2	0	0	1	2	1	1	0	0	2
Venus	3	3	0	1	0	1	3	1	0	0	1	0
Saturn	2	2	2	3	0	0	0	0	5	0	1	0

After Ekadhipatya Shodhyan (Reduction)

Planets	1	2	3	4	5	6	7	8	9	10	11	12
Sun	3	1	4	1	0	0	0	0	1	0	3	1
Moon	2	0	1	0	0	3	0	2	1	0	0	1
Mars	0	4	1	1	0	2	0	1	0	0	3	0
Mercury	4	2	0	2	2	2	2	0	0	0	4	0
Jupiter	0	0	2	0	0	1	0	1	1	0	0	1
Venus	1	0	0	1	0	1	0	1	0	0	1	0
Saturn	2	2	2	3	0	0	0	0	5	0	1	0

Shodhya Pinda

Planets	Sun	Moon	Mars	Mercury	Jupiter	Venus	Saturn
Rashi Pinda	121	74	103	144	50	35	118
Graha Pinda	37	50	52	80	25	32	61
Total	**158**	**124**	**155**	**224**	**75**	**67**	**179**

4   Sachin Tendulkar

DOB: 21-04-1973 TOB: 18-01-00 Hrs POB: Mumbai

North Indian chart	South Indian chart

(North Indian chart, left:)
- 7 / 8 Mon / Asc
- 5 / 4
- 6 / 3 Ket
- 9 / 12
- Rah
- Jup Mar 10 / 11
- Mer
- 2 Sat / 1
- Sun Ven

(South Indian chart, right:)

Mer	Sun Ven	Sat	Ket
	24-01-1933		
Jup Mar			
Rah	Mon		Asc

Bhinnashtakvarga

Planets	1	2	3	4	5	6	7	8	9	10	11	12
Sun	3	4	3	4	5	4	3	6	4	5	5	2
Moon	2	3	5	5	3	5	6	5	3	5	4	3
Mars	2	2	3	3	4	4	2	5	2	5	5	2
Mercury	4	3	5	4	7	4	2	5	7	3	7	3
Jupiter	5	4	3	7	4	4	5	4	5	6	5	4
Venus	2	5	3	5	4	5	3	7	5	5	4	4
Saturn	2	3	3	3	1	4	4	5	4	3	4	3
Total	20	24	25	31	28	30	25	37	30	32	34	21

After Trikona Shodhyan (Reduction)

Planets	1	2	3	4	5	6	7	8	9	10	11	12
Sun	0	0	0	2	2	0	0	4	1	1	2	0
Moon	0	0	1	2	1	2	2	2	1	2	0	0
Mars	0	0	1	1	2	2	0	3	0	3	3	0
Mercury	0	0	3	1	3	1	0	2	3	0	5	0
Jupiter	1	0	0	3	0	0	2	0	1	2	2	0
Venus	0	0	0	1	2	0	0	3	3	0	1	0
Saturn	2	0	0	0	0	1	1	2	3	0	1	0

After Ekadhipatya Shodhyan (Reduction)

Planets	1	2	3	4	5	6	7	8	9	10	11	12
Sun	0	0	0	2	2	0	0	4	1	1	1	0
Moon	0	0	0	2	1	2	2	2	1	2	0	0
Mars	0	0	0	1	2	2	0	3	0	3	0	0
Mercury	0	0	1	1	3	1	0	2	3	0	5	0
Jupiter	1	0	0	3	0	0	2	0	1	2	0	0
Venus	0	0	0	1	2	0	0	3	3	0	1	0
Saturn	1	0	0	0	0	1	1	2	3	0	1	0

Shodhya Pinda

Planets	Sun	Moon	Mars	Mercury	Jupiter	Venus	Saturn
Rashi Pinda	85	77	73	145	52	86	73
Graha Pinda	38	46	69	10	48	15	22
Total	**123**	**123**	**142**	**155**	**100**	**101**	**95**

5 Lal Bahadur Shastri

DOB: 09-10-1904 TOB: 10-46-20 Hrs POB: Varanasi

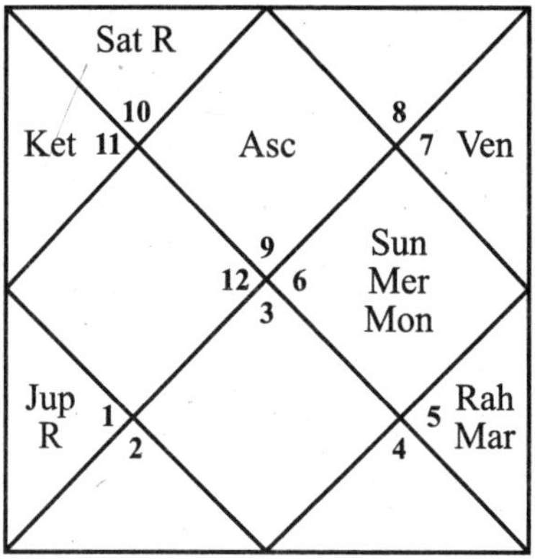
Sat R
Ket 11
10
Asc
8
7 Ven
9
12
6
3
Sun
Mer
Mon
Jup
R
1
2
4
5
Rah
Mar

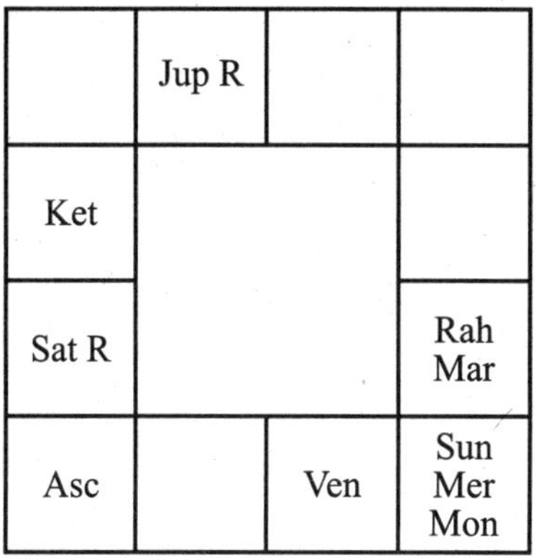
Jup R
Ket
Sat R
Rah
Mar
Asc
Ven
Sun
Mer
Mon

Bhinnashtakvarga

Planets	**1**	**2**	**3**	**4**	**5**	**6**	**7**	**8**	**9**	**10**	**11**	**12**
Sun	4	4	4	4	4	6	3	5	2	2	6	4
Moon	5	3	6	5	1	4	3	5	3	4	5	5
Mars	1	3	2	4	3	5	2	5	1	4	6	3
Mercury	3	5	4	5	5	5	4	5	3	5	7	3
Jupiter	3	7	7	5	3	4	5	4	4	4	4	6
Venus	5	4	2	6	6	2	5	5	5	6	4	2
Saturn	2	4	4	4	3	4	3	2	3	1	4	5
Total	**23**	**30**	**29**	**33**	**25**	**30**	**25**	**31**	**21**	**26**	**36**	**28**

After Trikona Shodhyan (Reduction)

Planets	1	2	3	4	5	6	7	8	9	10	11	12
Sun	2	2	1	0	2	4	0	1	0	0	3	0
Moon	4	0	3	0	0	1	0	0	2	1	2	0
Mars	0	0	0	1	2	2	0	2	0	1	4	0
Mercury	0	0	0	2	2	0	0	2	0	0	3	0
Jupiter	0	3	3	1	0	0	1	0	1	0	0	2
Venus	0	2	0	4	1	0	3	3	0	4	2	0
Saturn	0	3	1	2	1	3	0	0	1	0	1	3

After Ekadhipatya Shodhyan (Reduction)

Planets	1	2	3	4	5	6	7	8	9	10	11	12
Sun	2	2	0	0	2	4	0	0	0	0	3	0
Moon	4	0	1	0	0	1	0	0	2	1	1	0
Mars	0	0	0	1	2	2	0	2	0	1	1	0
Mercury	0	0	0	2	2	0	0	2	0	0	3	0
Jupiter	0	1	3	1	0	0	1	0	1	0	0	1
Venus	0	0	0	4	1	0	3	3	0	4	0	0
Saturn	0	3	0	2	1	3	0	0	1	0	1	1

Shodhya Pinda

Planets	Sun	Moon	Mars	Mercury	Jupiter	Venus	Saturn
Rashi Pinda	107	75	66	77	66	91	95
Graha Pinda	96	60	51	16	07	49	53
Total	**203**	**135**	**117**	**93**	**73**	**140**	**148**

6   Sanjay Gandhi

DOB: 14-12-1946 TOB: 09-27-00 Hrs POB: Delhi

Bhinnashtakvarga

Planets	1	2	3	4	5	6	7	8	9	10	11	12
Sun	4	3	5	4	5	4	5	2	3	4	3	6
Moon	4	6	5	2	6	5	4	3	2	6	4	2
Mars	3	2	3	3	3	5	4	1	1	6	1	7
Mercury	4	4	4	4	6	5	6	4	2	6	3	6
Jupiter	4	3	6	6	4	6	3	6	6	4	5	3
Venus	5	5	4	4	5	5	5	5	2	3	5	4
Saturn	3	3	4	1	4	6	4	4	2	2	3	3
Total	**27**	**26**	**31**	**24**	**33**	**36**	**31**	**25**	**18**	**31**	**24**	**31**

After Trikona Shodhyan (Reduction)

Planets	1	2	3	4	5	6	7	8	9	10	11	12
Sun	1	0	2	2	2	1	2	0	0	1	0	4
Moon	2	1	1	0	4	0	0	1	0	1	0	0
Mars	2	0	2	2	2	3	3	0	0	4	0	6
Mercury	2	0	1	0	4	1	3	0	0	2	0	2
Jupiter	0	0	3	3	0	3	0	3	2	1	2	0
Venus	3	2	0	0	3	2	1	1	0	0	1	0
Saturn	1	1	1	0	2	4	1	3	0	0	0	2

After Ekadhipatya Shodhyan (Reduction)

Planets	1	2	3	4	5	6	7	8	9	10	11	12
Sun	1	0	1	2	2	1	2	0	0	1	0	4
Moon	1	1	1	0	4	0	0	1	0	1	0	0
Mars	2	0	2	2	2	2	3	0	0	4	0	6
Mercury	2	0	0	0	4	0	3	0	0	2	0	2
Jupiter	0	0	0	3	0	0	0	3	2	1	1	0
Venus	1	1	0	0	3	2	1	1	0	0	1	0
Saturn	0	0	1	0	2	1	1	3	0	0	0	2

Shodhya Pinda

Planets	Sun	Moon	Mars	Mercury	Jupiter	Venus	Saturn
Rashi Pinda	115	78	181	109	70	83	88
Graha Pinda	54	30	71	71	61	42	57
Total	**169**	**108**	**252**	**180**	**131**	**125**	**145**

Exercises Horoscopes: Do it yourself

7   J. L. Nehru

DOB: 14-11-1889 TOB: 11-03-00 Hrs POB: Allahabad

Bhinnashtakvarga

Planets	1	2	3	4	5	6	7	8	9	10	11	12
Sun	6	6	5	3	4	7	3	2	5	0	3	4
Moon	5	5	5	5	3	4	4	2	6	6	3	1
Mars	4	5	2	2	4	6	2	2	4	1	2	5
Mercury	5	6	4	5	5	4	7	3	5	1	5	4
Jupiter	2	3	5	7	5	3	5	5	5	6	4	6
Venus	2	5	5	5	6	4	6	5	3	2	5	4
Saturn	2	5	4	3	4	5	3	3	4	2	2	2
Total	**26**	**35**	**30**	**30**	**31**	**33**	**30**	**22**	**32**	**18**	**24**	**26**

Shodhya Pinda

Planets	Sun	Moon	Mars	Mercury	Jupiter	Venus	Saturn
Rashi Pinda	134	91	101	97	95	88	82
Graha Pinda	71	67	40	70	67	68	76
Total	205	158	141	167	162	156	158

8.   Atal Behari Bajpai

DOB: 25-12-1924 TOB: 05-15-00 Hrs POB: Gawalior

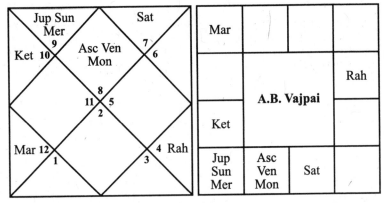

Bhinnashtakvarga

Planets	1	2	3	4	5	6	7	8	9	10	11	12
Sun	7	4	3	2	6	5	7	3	2	5	2	2
Moon	4	4	3	5	5	6	3	3	4	4	4	4
Mars	7	4	3	1	2	6	6	2	4	4	2	1
Mercury	6	4	5	3	5	5	5	7	5	3	4	2
Jupiter	4	3	3	5	4	8	4	4	8	4	4	8
Venus	2	3	4	7	5	4	4	5	4	5	6	3
Saturn	4	3	1	3	4	5	4	3	3	4	3	2
Total	34	25	22	26	31	39	33	24	27	29	25	22

Shodhya Pinda

Planets	Sun	Moon	Mars	Mercury	Jupiter	Venus	Saturn
Rashi Pinda	95	51	66	64	168	85	69
Graha Pinda	37	08	32	65	141	64	27
Total	**132**	**59**	**98**	**129**	**309**	**149**	**96**

9   Rajiv Gandhi

DOB: 20-08-1944 TOB: 08-11-40 Hrs   POB: Mumbai

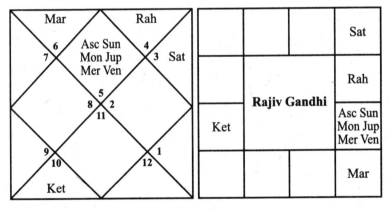

Bhinnashtakvarga

Planets	1	2	3	4	5	6	7	8	9	10	11	12
Sun	5	5	7	5	1	3	4	2	4	6	3	3
Moon	2	7	7	2	4	0	7	5	2	4	6	3
Mars	2	3	8	3	1	2	5	0	4	7	1	3
Mercury	5	4	8	5	3	5	3	3	5	6	1	6
Jupiter	6	6	7	1	5	7	4	5	5	3	4	3
Venus	6	3	6	3	5	4	5	4	5	3	2	6
Saturn	2	3	7	4	4	1	3	4	1	6	2	2
Total	**28**	**31**	**50**	**23**	**23**	**22**	**31**	**23**	**26**	**35**	**19**	**26**

Shodhya Pinda

Planets	Sun	Moon	Mars	Mercury	Jupiter	Venus	Saturn
Rashi Pinda	125	101	117	149	113	94	135
Graha Pinda	20	69	35	43	47	28	121
Total	**145**	**170**	**152**	**192**	**160**	**122**	**256**

Sarvashtakvarga and its Shodhya Pinda

10. Amitabh Bachhan

DOB: 11-10-1942 TOB: 15-01-36 Hrs POB: Allahabad

		Sat R		27	26	33	29
Asc Ket	**Amitabh Bachhan**	Jup	31 Lag	**SAV**		42
		Rah	24			23
	Mon	Sun Mar Mer Ven	32	29	21	20

Shodhya Pinda

Planets	Sun	Moon	Mars	Mercury	Jupiter	Venus	Saturn	**Total**
Graha Pinda	0	20	0	0	30	0	5	**55**

Rashi Pinda

Rashi	1	2	3	4	5	6	7	8	9	10	11	12	Total
Rashi Pinda	0	10	0	12	90	0	28	16	54	10	22	0	242

Graha Pinda: 55 + 242 = 297